The most effective help for our society's most pervasive ills—from alcoholism to criminality, from drug addiction to obesity —has come not from professionals but from ordinary people banding together to help themselves. In recent years, hundreds of these self-help groups have come to the fore.

What principles undergird these groups? What is their historical setting? How do they actually work? And what do groups and professionals have to say to one another?

John Drakeford, a psychologist who has worked for over thirteen years with self-help groups, here tells where they came from, how they work, and, as important, *why* they work.

The roots of people to people therapy are diverse. John Wesley, the founder of Methodism; Frank Buchman, who launched the Oxford Group Movement; Bill W., who began Alcoholics Anonymous; and many more—all played significant roles in the development of this therapeutic style. Dr. Drakeford shows what each contributed to our understanding of groups and of how they work.

How *do* they work? *People to People Therapy* indicates in complete detail how members come to groups, techniques for bringing a group to birth, ground rules for effectively moving groups along, and ways to avoid the emotional dangers of group life. It lists and analyzes the principles common to most self-helpers. There are even "Ideas for Group Facilitators" at the end of every chapter that give people who work with groups new approaches and structured experiences for use in group activities. And specific case examples bring the principles home to real-life situations.

Assuaging professionals' fears and answering skepticism, *People to People Therapy* offers practical advice on forming and maintaining groups. In it, John Drakeford has provided the single most complete guide to people helping people transform their lives.

John W. Drakeford is Professor of Psychology and Counseling at Southwestern Baptist Theological Seminary in Fort Worth, Texas. Dr. Drakeford is also the Director of the Baptist Marriage and Family Counseling Center, where he has worked with self-help groups for many years. He has written twenty-three books, including *Integrity Therapy* and *"Do You Hear Me, Honey?"*

People to People Therapy

People to
People Therapy

JOHN W. DRAKEFORD

Published in San Francisco by

HARPER & ROW, PUBLISHERS

1817

New York, Hagerstown, London, San Francisco

1817

PEOPLE TO PEOPLE THERAPY. Copyright © 1978 by John W. Drakeford.
All rights reserved. Printed in the United States of America. No part of
this book may be used or reproduced in any manner whatsoever without
written permission except in the case of brief quotations embodied in
critical articles and reviews. For information address Harper & Row,
Publishers, Inc., 10 East 53rd Street, New York, N.Y. 10022. Published
simultaneously in Canada by Fitzhenry & Whiteside Limited, Toronto.

FIRST EDITION

Designed by Jim Mennick

Library of Congress Cataloging in Publication Data

Drakeford, John W.
   PEOPLE TO PEOPLE THERAPY.

   Includes index.
   1. Group psychotherapy. I. Title.
RC488.D7   616.8′915   77-20447
ISBN 0-06-062062-5

78 79 80 81 82 10 9 8 7 6 5 4 3 2 1

Contents

Preface

IT ALL started when a psychiatrist complained. We were sitting in the officer's mess and the psychiatrist was lamenting the overload of work in his ward. In this World War II era, soldiers with what were labeled emotional problems were being sent back from the Pacific islands in great numbers, and this conscientious medico had so many patients to care for that the situation had grown intolerable.

In the midst of a recital of his frustrations, the psychiatrist turned on me—"If you padres would only help us you could lighten the load."—So the next morning I presented myself at his office. He pulled some folders from his filing cabinet. "Here are three cases. See what you can do with them. You can't do much worse than us. You may do better." Thus began a pleasant and profitable association that helped me realize I could embark on a counseling ministry to assist troubled people.

Later I developed an academic interest in counseling as I piled up psychology course on psychology course, and moved into teaching the subject. In the process I founded a counseling center as a teaching clinic for my students. It has continued to grow and now, some eighteen years later, is a healthy, vigorous enterprise.

The year 1964 was the watershed. I received a grant from the Eli Lilly Foundation and became a Lilly Fellow studying under Dr. O. Hobart Mowrer. Dr. Mowrer had been a National Research Fellow at Northwestern and Princeton Universities, President of the American Psychological Association, author of a number of influential books, and was at this time Research Professor, Psychology Department, University of Illinois. This unusual man had written two books, *The Crisis in Psychiatry and Religion* (New York: Van Nostrand, 1961) and *The New Group Therapy* (New York: Van Nostrand, 1964), in which he had presented the theory that an individual's failure to live by his or her values led to secrecy and malaise and that the way back to healthy adjustment was to accept responsibility, become open first with one person and then with a group, and move on to helping other people. I was not convinced at first, as he challenged many of the ideas I'd held for so long. In our disputes Mowrer had one powerful factor going for him—his theory worked. My work with him involved spending one day a week working with groups at the State Research Hospital in Galesburg, Illinois. As I worked with Mowrer and participated in the patient groups, I finally accepted the logic of his theory. By a happy chance I was a member of a group traveling to the hospital when it was suggested that some name should be given to the theory and practice we were using. We reached a happy unanimity about the word *integrity*.

After a return to the counseling center, during which I went through the difficult experience of changing the operation from individual to group therapy, I watched the enterprise blossom. Three years of experience led to my book *Integrity Therapy* (Nashville: Broadman, 1967). In a sense *People to People Therapy* is a sequel to *Integrity Therapy*, with a major emphasis on the group process. It is written in the hope that a great many people will catch the vision, put it into practice, and so prove they are not afraid of the self-help groups.

JOHN W. DRAKEFORD

Fort Worth, Texas
October 27, 1977

Introduction:
Here Come the
Nonprofessionals

THE YEAR 1793 could have been the most brilliant in Philadelphia's history, as the city then occupied the position of temporary capital of the United States of America. Instead, it turned into a summer of horror as the city of brotherly love witnessed some of the most heart-rending scenes of human suffering ever experienced in America. Within a short four-month period, a yellow fever plague decimated the population by killing off 10 percent of the citizenry.

Dr. Benjamin Rush, probably the most outstanding medical personality of that day and a man already assured of a place in history by his signing of the Declaration of Independence, threw himself into the task of helping his unfortunate fellow citizens. In the strange elation that comes from commitment to such an enterprise, he wrote, "Never was the healing art so delightful to me."

Periodically Rush met with the prestigious College of Physicians, which consisted of sixteen physicians who speculated and argued about the cause and cure of the disease without coming close to either. J. H. Powell, historian of the yellow fever epidemic in Philadelphia in 1793, suggests that because they were gentlemen scientists, they were removed from close contact with the early events of the 1793 plague. The "quacks," midwives, nurses, aurists, apothecaries, and barber-surgeons were much closer to the sufferers and might have provided the best information for evaluating the pestilence.

In the early days of the epidemic, a citizen of the city wrote a letter to *Dunlap's American Daily Advertiser.* He signed himself *A.B.* and made the rather mundane suggestion that rainbarrels provided breeding places for mosquitoes, which were poisonous and distressing. He proposed that a wine glass of oil poured on the water would cover it with a film and prevent mosquitoes breeding.

The problem was that A.B. was only an ignorant layperson. Yet had his suggestion been followed, a hundred years of human misery might have been averted. The cities of Baltimore, Mobile, and New Orleans might have been saved from the agony of yellow fever. If yellow fever had not frustrated the efforts of de Lessepts, the Panama Canal could have become a French waterway. Had Philadelphia's leaders listened to A.B.'s suggestion, the course of history might have been changed.

The professionals excelled in one area—they were very precise in their descriptions of the disease. Their commitment to research led them to turn aside from the urgent task of treating the sick and to do postmortems. They wrote voluminously about the effects of the disease on the human body. But in two areas they failed completely. They discovered neither the cause nor the cure, both of far greater significance than the more detailed descriptions of symptoms and effects.

Benjamin Rush is also known as the father of American psychiatry, and he was as opinionated in his speculations about mental illness as in his theories of yellow fever. He wrote the first systematic treatment of psychiatry in his book *Medical Inquiries and Observations Upon Diseases of the Mind,* and organized the first course in the study of psychiatry. Rush offered much the same remedies for mental illness as he had for yellow fever, namely, purgatives and bloodletting. To these he added a "gyrator" to increase cerebral circulation, and a "tranquilizer," which device made the patient's head as immovable as the Rock of Gibraltar.

Rush's diagnostic dilemmas may be the quandary of the social scientists today. There are vast quantities of research that describe in intricate detail the manifestations of alcoholism, drug addiction, and criminal behavior, and the neurosis and psychosis. Elaborate classifications make it possible to pinpoint accurately and name the difficulty. But most of this work is descriptive, with little to say about the real cause and cure. And, as in Rush's day, the professionals have a proprietary attitude in these fields and frequently infer that interested laypeople may only exacerbate the situation with their meddling.

Letter writer A.B. became as annoying to the newspapers as those obnoxious mosquitoes that ruined the sleep of sweltering Philadelphians. One stinging letter he wrote to the *Federal Gazette* poured scorn on the practice of lighting fires in front of houses and on street corners; it had already proved ineffective for controlling infectious disorders in London and Charleston. Another letter by A.B. complained about the practice of tolling church bells at the news of a death because the doleful bells depressed the sick.

This gadfly was a keen observer. From what he saw he drew conclusions as to the cause and cure of the fever. His practical suggestion of pouring oil on water in the rainbarrels that provided a breeding place for mosquitoes, which, in turn, "poisoned" the people were of much greater value than all the combined theoretical speculations of the professionals. As one commentator remarks, "He spelled out the source of the trouble and the remedy with pinpoint accuracy."[1] One hundred years later, Dr. Walter Reed showed by a practical experiment the viability of A.B.'s ideas.

The modern equivalent of A.B. is the nonprofessional who, blissfully ignorant of many of the scientific investigations and the detailed descriptions of the social scientists, has become a part of a powerful self-help group that produces almost miraculous results. Within this setting troubled people have found a way by learning to accept personal responsibility and walk a pathway of meaningful living. By practical activity, self-help groups have demonstrated the validity of their underlying philosophies.

The whole new stress on community mental-health projects is an acknowledgment of the necessity of keeping troubled people in their normal social context. Commitment to a detached institution may have meant a safe and secure refuge far removed from life, sometimes leading to a condition characterized as *institutionalized*. But living in this little sheltered world, the inmate settles down with many basic motivations for recovery lost.

If community programs are to provide help for the vast number of needy people, the work can never be done by professionals alone. Lay men and women must be enlisted in the process. We may discover that not only will they supply extra help, in some instances they may even be more effective than the professionals they replace.

The situation we are facing today is generally presented in a scenario that goes like this: In an age of increasingly complex technology when so many people feel rootless, lonely, and unwanted, we need a new, highly developed form of psychotherapy with highly trained professionals who can utilize the fruits of scientific research to help heal the hurt of men and women. Well, perhaps. If we accept the experiences of the peer mutual self-help psychotherapy groups, we may have to return to a simpler approach to the problem of helping troubled people.

Many of the problems people find most troublesome, such as alcoholism, drug addiction, obesity, antisocial behavior, and neurotic distress, have been stubbornly resistant to the best efforts of professionals in the behavioral sciences. Yet these are the very areas in which the peer mutual self-help psychotherapy groups have been most successful. One psychoanalyst who has had a wide experience in work with alcoholics says, "Probably the most effective treatment we have is that of Alcoholics Anonymous." Two other professionals reporting on people addicted to narcotics, dangerous drugs, and alcohol state, "Of the 860 who have come to Synanon, 55 percent have stayed and kept free of addiction even though the door is open at all times."[2] The same story could be reported many times over in the areas of obesity, neurosis, criminal behavior, and so on. The great success of the self-help groups has not been in the so-called simple problems of life but in the areas that are most complex and difficult to control.

Once when a colleague had been discussing a problem and I suggested what I considered a rather elementary solution, my friend responded, "Trust the old pro to come up with an answer." That phrase *old pro* brought a warmth to me at the time, but later on and with maturer consideration I wondered if that was what I really wanted to be. We have entered into an era in sports, for example, in which we have become a generation of spectators rather than participants, urging on the adept athletes and paying them a good rate if they perform well, and all the while concerned about our own ailments associated with lack of exercise. An absence of involvement seems to be the attitude of our age.

The exaltation of professionals has often meant that we have some unrealistic ideas about them as individuals. One physician participating in the discussion of medical services called for a new participation by patients. He obliquely referred to the attitude of the professionals by remarking, "Patients will have to get up off their knees and quit worshiping their doctor."

Professionalism demands training. So the professional educators increase the number of courses to provide the basics for the would-be professional. Then come supervised experiences, where those who have managed to gain some status rather condescendingly undertake to initiate the neophyte into the mystique of the discipline. These are followed, in turn, by the boards and professional organizations that hand out credentials to those who can pass the examinations and fulfill the professional requirements. Professional organizations abound; to be a full-fledged member in some professions involves a considerable outlay of money and time. Such activities are alleged to be geared toward delivering better services to the client, but in actual fact there are some pretty good reasons for doubting this claim. On closer examination it seems that the main function of many of these organizations is to create a "closed shop" by limiting the number of competitors and thus ensuring a good flow of clients for the "approved." All too frequently troubled individuals find themselves paying exorbitant fees for the services of a complacent, bored professional who gives every indication of having an interest that is mainly financial.

Commenting on the peer mutual self-help psychotherapy groups, Anthony J. Vattano makes the point in "Self-Help Groups: Power to the People" that self-help groups may represent the emergence of the spirit of egalitarianism, which says members of the community have an ability to help each other. This spirit is manifesting itself in self-helpers as they try to help each other with emotional and behavioral problems.[3]

Vattano suggests a number of factors that have gone into producing self-help groups:

1. As the population has grown, health and welfare services have failed to keep pace; consequently there are not enough professionals to meet the demands for help.

2. Evidence is mounting to show that the social and clinical services that are available have not been very effective.

3. Many of the traditional credentials and authorities are coming under question, and a sense is developing that common people may have more abilities than they have been credited with.

4. Self-help groups have been effective in some of the particularly stubborn problems of human personality, such as alcoholism and drug addiction.

5. In a rapidly changing society in which many of the fruits of technology have been somewhat disappointing, many people are leaning toward deciding their own destiny rather than trusting it to other people.[4]

Discussion of self-help groups emphasizes the words *peer* and *mutual*, indicating that they function apart from professionals. Some of these groups are almost opposed to professionals; Alcoholics Anonymous, for instance, openly states, "A.A. shall forever remain nonprofessional." This seems to be the general attitude of self-helpers toward professionals.

Professionals and self-helpers have an ambivalent relationship. Vattano indicates this when he discusses professional leadership and says, "In clinical self-help groups professional leadership is either absent (e.g., Alcoholics Anonymous), shared with members of the group (e.g., Integrity Groups), replaced by peer role models (e.g., Synanon)."[5]

This nonprofessional aspect of the peer self-help psychotherapy groups has been recognized by sympathetic professionals who wished to use their undoubted abilities in helping people. Nathan Hurvitz suggests professionals might help to set up a self-help group, but he notes how necessary it is for the professional to "get out of the way" of the group. If professionals stay around, they may only succeed in thwarting the group's function.

Unfortunately the success of many of these peer mutual self-help psychotherapy groups has caused many professionals to adopt attitudes toward them that are sometimes hostile, sometimes condescending, and in other instances damning with faint praise. The peer mutual self-help psychotherapy groups, for their part, have all too frequently had a less than positive attitude toward professionals, feeling that by and large they don't know much about what they're doing and are content to make a good living from human misery. Considering the number of people needing help, this situation is deplorable. Some method of compromise must be found.

V. Edwin Bixenstine has presented a model in which he sees professionals combining with the peer mutual self-help psychotherapy groups.[6] He describes an experiment in Canton, Ohio where a community house was established. The house was run by a board to which the professionals were subordinated. In the total functioning of the enterprise, the professionals were to be participating members. Bixenstine himself was the staff psychologist and saw himself as resident-facilitator. He describes the way the board members and staff interacted with him and the other professionals:

1. They have come to value our "long view" and our knack for analysis so that we are used to help explain what has occurred and to predict likely outcomes of new programs.
2. They value our stores of knowledge and our facility with concepts. We have been especially relied on in shaping in-house training programs for member leaders. The language, rationale and idiomatic culture of Community House bears a heavy imprint of our judgment.
3. Members and staff depend on us to help evaluate, measure and describe change processes and to conduct any necessary statistical analyses.
4. While other persons are also participating, we are especially relied upon to "trouble shoot" and to take part in helping resolve internal conflicts. Again our analytic and conceptual talents are employed, but conflict resolution depends more in the end on the appeal to group loyalty and emotional investment in shared goals.
5. They call on us to run interference in relation with other, potentially unfriendly professionals outside Community House. We "legitimate" the enterprise for many persons and enable them to accept or at least not oppose Community House (though they often misunderstand it and our role in it).
6. Finally, I have had a unique role owing to my part in helping to establish Community House and to my part as peer-member. It is difficult to clearly describe this aspect of my status. It involves respect sometimes bordering on awe, affection, gratitude—rueful tolerance for my idiosyncracies (e.g., forgetfulness). Perhaps this constitutes a transformation of the professionally impersonal "consultant-facilitator": into the personal, more valued "kindly wise man" who might have emerged regardless of my association with the enterprise.[7]

Other professionals are increasingly coming to welcome the work of the self-helpers. Dr. Walt Menninger, a representative of the mainstream of the professional psychiatric establishment, has recently written in glowing terms about the work of the self-helpers and highlighted such organizations as Recovery, Inc., and Emotional Health Anonymous. After a warm commendation of Recovery he notes, "A key to the self-help [groups] is nonprofessional leadership," and notes that while mental health professionals are welcome to attend Recovery meetings and participate as members, "they are specifically denied leadership roles." Dr. Menninger states his position:

> As a mental health professional, I heartily salute the efforts of these organizations. Dr. Low started Recovery, Inc., because he was keenly aware that there were many more people in need of help than professionals to provide that help. These organizations have been and will certainly continue supplementing and complementing services available from mental health professionals.[8]

It is my prediction the self-help groups will continue to proliferate and in many instances bypass the more orthodox professional in the field of mental health. Obviously, the most profitable thing for all would be for professionals and self-helpers to get together. We must acknowledge that the professionals have found the self-helpers not only self-confident and lacking in respect for professional expertise but somewhat vague about their theoretical undergirdings; thus it is difficult for the professionals to get a handle on them. The self-helpers, being interested in action and geting on with the job, have not bothered too much about formulating the theoretical basis of their function. When I personally became interested in the self-help groups, I had to set up arbitrary criteria, which I did in my book *Farewell to the Lonely Crowd* (Waco, Texas: Word Books, 1969). Now after years of working with one group, I am ready to suggest the following criteria by which to judge a self-help group. We may say that self-help groups:

1. Utilize nonprofessional leaders. Sometimes they are even suspicious of highly trained professionals.

2. Emphasize personal responsibility. They won't allow people to blame the past or the influence of others for their problems.

3. Maintain high standards. They will not let participants offer good excuses for bad behavior.

4. Provide a setting for and encourage self-disclosure. Most of them emphasize some form of confession.

5. Use distinctive techniques of teaching and inspiration. These may include slogans or songs.

6. Motivate participants into action. They refuse to let members speculate about insights or causes, but insist they *do* something.

7. Utilize peer groups. "Like speaks to like" is a basic concept.

After the experience of working with Dr. O. Hobart Mowrer, I launched into a new era of professional activity and have for some twelve years been involved with groups generally known as Integrity Therapy groups, slightly different in name and practice from Dr. Mowrer's Integrity groups but operating on the same general principles. These groups involve an intermingling of professionals and nonprofessionals but are committed to training lay people who will become facilitators of self-help groups.

This book is written with the hope of fostering the developing interest in peer mutual self-help psychotherapy groups by showing something of the background from which they have come, exploring the principles upon which they are built, and then examining the operations of the Integrity Therapy group, indicating its processes and procedures.

ROOTS

At this moment we are witnessing a resurgence of interest in people's antecedents. Aided and abetted by a spate of books, movies, and television programs, many are under the spell of the idea that "If you don't know where you've been, you can't tell where you are going." Looking into the background of self-help groups, we discover they have a short history but a long past, and in that past some surprising people were instrumental in their development.

≋ 1. An Unlikely Pioneer

A NEW chapter in Australian history was written in the nineteenth century when two explorers, Robert O'Hara Burke and William Gorman Wills by name, led an ill-fated expedition seeking to find a route from the south to the north of the Australian continent. Imagine my delight as I read the story of the heroic effort when I discovered one member of their party was a man named John Drakeford. At last a possible ancestor had made his mark on history's page. As the story moved on, however, my family pride took a beating. It turned out John Drakeford, the cook, was an alcoholic, notoriously unreliable, who finally deserted the expedition and headed back to civilization and the solace of the bottle. Any excursion into the past has a strange potential for turning up unexpected and somewhat embarrassing ancestry. Such may be the case with the self-help groups.

Speculations about who might have been the originator of group therapy have taken some strange turns, with a good number of authorities naming Dr. J. H. Pratt for his efforts with tuberculosis patients in the Boston dispensary in 1905. While investigating early groups and their origins, I frequently ran across references to an organization called the Methodist Class Meeting, where people gathered for experiences of interaction and relationship. As I looked into this organization, I came upon a series of clues pointing toward some intensive group activity hardly ever mentioned in the literature on groups, and associated with the name of John Wesley, the founder of Methodism.

Wesley proved to be a fascinating subject for research, in part because he was a compulsive diarist who not only recorded thoughts about the passing scene, including a warning to the rebellious American colonists, but also gave detailed reports of his daily activities—what time he arose and retired, what he did, where he went (he traveled between four and five thousand miles each year), how he felt ("I entered into the 83rd year of my age. I'm a wonder to myself. It's now 12 years since I have felt any sensation such as weariness."), and a very precise description of the organizations he developed.

As he observed the people who gathered around him, Wesley painstakingly recorded their reactions. For instance, as he was preaching a sermon, several members of the congregation cried out with a loud voice and fell to the floor. Wesley visited these people in their homes and plied them with questions. What was the condition of their health? Most of them were in perfect health and not subject to fits. In what way did it happen? It came upon them suddenly, without any anticipation. And so on. Wesley's penchant for examining human reactions has given us some excellent material for further study.

Another advantage of studying Wesley is that he spent a lot of time ferreting out information about primitive Christianity. Speaking of one aspect of Methodist life he said, "Upon reflection, I saw how exactly we had copied the primitive church." From these and other statements, he made it clear he tried to fashion the life of his new movement upon that of the early church. His groups thus become a bridge to the primitive church, which carried on much of its work through small groups.

A small, austere, but neatly dressed little man, with a rather prominent nose, John Wesley spent his days as a priest of the Anglican church. He entered the world in the Church of England rectory at Epworth on June 17, 1703, and eighty-eight years later, March 2, 1791, surrounded by a group of people in a room of a house in City Road, London, he closed his eyes for the last time. During these eighty-eight years Wesley's remarkable ministry proceeded on three fronts, with the practice of fervent evangelism, a program of social concerns, and the unique use of group dynamics.

His interest in evangelism came from his personal experience, and he engaged in a passionate preaching crusade in churches, town squares, and anywhere he could assemble a group of people. Wesley's interest in people's souls did not blind him to their everyday needs. As his work progressed he organized schools, dispensaries, and employment schemes for the unfortunates of eighteenth-century England. Social concerns loomed large in all the activities of Wesley's organization.

Wesley's third emphasis was his insistence on the importance of experiences of association or affiliation. This concern probably stemmed back to his own experiences. Born into a large family, he had plunged into its varied activity and learned many valuable lessons under the capable tutelage of his mother Susannah, who was a group leader par excellence.

When he commenced his religious quest in his late teens, Wesley was under the sway of the mystics. He had spent much time reading William Law's *Serious Call to a Devout Life* and *Christian Perfection* and other mystical writings, and he became an ardent admirer of the mystics. It seemed to him that the heart of religion was the quest of a lonely soul for a lonely God. People around him distracted him from the quest. Their talk of mundane everyday affairs was so trivial that it eroded the interest in a deep and difficult communion with the Eternal. Before he could spend time in fellowship with other people, he must be sure of his relationship with his God.

During an interlude in his career at Oxford University, Wesley spent time serving the Anglican church at Wroote. While working among the people of the marshy fenlands, he came into contact with Rev. Hoole, Rector of Haxey. As the serious-minded young minister talked about finding God for oneself, Hoole replied, "Sir, you wish to serve God and go to Heaven? Remember you cannot serve Him alone. You must try to find companions or make them. The Bible knows nothing of solitary religion."[1]

This conversation led Wesley to a new religious perspective. It became very clear to him now that he could not hope to accomplish his mission as a recluse. Those awful lonely hours were not really necessary. There must be a fellowship of like-minded people. He began to plan ways in which he could practice his religion more effectively in the fellowship of those who shared his convictions and who would help to provoke him to good works.

A summons from Lincoln College in Oxford sent Wesley back to academic life. Here he found that his brother Charles had formed the Holy Club, and, newly aware of the importance of relationship with his fellows, John enthusiastically joined the group. The club followed a program of study, introspection, and religious activities; and a practical plan of visiting prisons, helping the sick, and bailing out the inmates of the debtors' prisons. Wesley became the leader of the group.

Dr. John Burton of Corpus Christi College, Oxford, introduced John Wesley to General Oglethorpe, the Governor of Georgia, newly returned from establishing the new British outpost. Oglethorpe was preparing for the Great Embarkation which would take a second group of immigrants to the new colony. Impressed with Wesley, Oglethorpe offered him the position of missionary. Wesley accepted Oglethorpe's invitation on the condition that he could take a team of three others with him. The group consisted of his brother Charles Wesley, destined to become the great hymn writer of later days; Charles Delamotte, a layman, the son of a London sugar merchant; and Benjamin Ingham, a Church of England minister. The spirit of the group can best be seen in a resolution they made while at anchor off the Isle of Wight before beginning the voyage. The four men wrote a compact clear for all to see.

In the name of God, Amen! We, whose names are underwritten, being fully convinced that it is impossible, either to promote the work of God among the heathen without an entire union among ourselves, or that such a union should subsist, unless each one will give up his single judgment to that of the majority, do agree, by the help of God:—first, that none of us will undertake anything of importance without first proposing it to the other three;—secondly, that whenever our judgments differ, any one shall give up his single judgment or inclination to the others;—thirdly, that in case of an equality, after begging God's direction, the matter shall be decided by lot.

John Wesley
Charles Wesley
Benjamin Ingham
Charles Delamotte[2]

This remarkable document shows that the expedition to Georgia carried on the spirit of the Holy Club and brought a tighter and more closely knit fellowship than the group had ever known before. However, this solemn covenant was to lead Wesley into one of his deepest problems during his troubled Georgian ministry.

While in Georgia Wesley gravitated more and more toward the group idea, gathering parishioners for informal discussions. He gradually developed a small group of people for the purpose of forming "a more intimate union with each other." Looking back later, he felt that the seeds of the groups he so successfully nurtured had been planted during these days.

Here, too, occurred the one incident that might have ruined Wesley's faith in the group process. This confirmed bachelor found himself increasingly drawn toward Sophie Hopkey, the niece of Thomas Causton, Savannah's chief magistrate. Concerned about losing their star bachelor member, the other members of the Club reminded him about his commitment in the Isle of Wight compact. By mutual agreement they decided to fast, pray, and draw lots to decide whether Wesley should marry Sophie. On one piece of paper they wrote "marry," on the second, "Think no more of it this year," and on the third, "Think of it no more." After prayer, the lot inscribed "Think of it no more" was drawn.

The group had reached the conclusion, and Wesley tried to accept the decision; but he suffered much internal agony over it. He broke with Sophie, who then married a Mr. Williamson, leaving Wesley so frustrated that he refused to give her communion. As a result, Sophie's uncle, in his role as chief magistrate of the colony, took the case to the grand jury, which concluded that Wesley had maligned Mrs. Williamson. To escape further legal action, Wesley fled Georgia and headed for Charleston, where he took a ship across the Atlantic to England.

The group's decision to separate him from the girl he loved might well have shattered Wesley's faith in groups, but it didn't. In fact, Wesley's return to England led him into more intensive involvement with groups. He helped to found a group known as the Fetter Lane Society. The rules of the Society contain some interesting statements, such as "We will meet together once a week to 'confess our faults one to another.'" One of the questions to prospective members was, "Will you be entirely open using no reserve?"[3] The basic theme of self-disclosure was to become a recurring note in the growing group movement.

While listening to a reading of Martin Luther's preface to the Epistle to the Romans at a meeting of another society in Aldersgate Street, Wesley felt his heart was "strangely warmed" and launched himself upon a new ministry. The peak experience in Aldersgate Street that lead to Wesley's continuing emphasis on evangelism took place on May 24, 1738. On June 14 Wesley crossed the channel to the continent to visit the Moravians. While on the voyage across the Atlantic to Georgia, during a storm at sea, the Moravians had impressed him by saying they were not afraid to die. When he returned to England the Moravian Peter Bohler had challenged Wesley to preach about faith. In the flush of his new found faith he felt the need to know more about these people who had influenced him so much and decided to visit the headquarters of their movement. He wrote about his visit at great length and described their organization in detail:

The people of Hernhuth are divided, 1. Into five male classes, viz., the little children, the middle children, the big children, the young men, and the married. The females are divided in the same manner. 2. Into eleven classes, according to the houses where they live: And in each class is an Helper, an Overseer, a Monitor, an Almoner, and a Servant. 3. Into about ninety bands, each of which meets twice at least, but most of them three times a week, to "confess their faults one to another, and pray for one another, that they may be healed."[4]

The image of this orderly pattern of life probably long remained in Wesley's mind.

Wesley had the administrator's temperament. In a letter to his sister he acknowledges the joy he felt in organizing groups: ". . . I know this is the peculiar talent which God has given me, wherein (by His grace) I am not behind the chiefest of them."[5] His remarkable organizations showed that he had not overestimated his ability.

It had all begun early in life. John Wesley was one of a family of nineteen children presided over by his remarkable mother, Susanna. This unusual woman, herself a product of a family of twenty-five children, organized her children and provided them with their elementary education. Her influence continued on Wesley throughout his ministry. When Wesley had reached a crucial point in his thinking about the role of the laity, Susanna urged him to remember the layman might be as much called of God as the ordained clergyman. In many ways a feminist before her time, she insisted her girls should get an elementary education before they learned any domestic skills. Later Wesley broke new ground by using women as leaders in his groups.

Wesley realized the importance of the family as the basic group in society and religious life. He urged his preachers to visit people in their homes. In their hands they carried literature especially prepared to educate the children in the fundamentals of their religious faith. The family was to be linked in with the foundational unit of Methodist life known as the Society. Other units of organization, such as the

Sunday school, sprang from this unit. Methodism moved forth on the feet of groups. Enquirers discovered that to seek to understand what Christianity was all about meant gathering with a group of people. If they had no great desire to be gregarious, Methodism was not for them. Methodism meant meetings, meetings, meetings. And once newcomers were incorporated into a fundamental grouping, pressures pushed them toward further commitments and more intimate relationships with their fellow believers.

John Wesley was a person prepared by temperament, inclination, and experience to study human personality. His experiences in groups strengthened a growing conviction about the validity of the group way as a means of helping people. In the following chapter we will see the way this conviction affected his work and led to the establishment of an unusual network of groups that provided for a wide variety of experiences.

≋ 2. Groups for All

JOHN WESLEY saw himself preeminently as an administrator within his organization, but he was also concerned about the personal lives of the individuals who were his followers. As he examined their spiritual maturity, he was frank enough to acknowledge, "Our religion is not deep, universal, uniform, but superficial, partial and uneven."[1] While he regretted this, he was realist enough to make provision for a variety of levels of group life into which Methodists could enter.

The groups were in a constant state of growth and development and it isn't always easy to understand how the various units related to each other. Speaking about the function of the lay assistants, Wesley made it clear that they would meet with the Society, the Class Meeting, the Bands, the Penitent Band, and the Select Society. The Society and Band both had trial groups, the Open Society and Trial Band, but the five groupings provided the basic structure for Wesleyan group life. An examination of these Wesleyan groups shows that they were formed on an experiential basis. Wesley's motto might well have been, "By their experience shall ye know them," and the level of experience determined the Methodist's place in group life (see Figure 1). To meet the needs of the people, each of these groups had a distinctive objective, membership requirements, and style of leadership, which we will examine in turn.

THE ASSOCIATION LEVEL–THE SOCIETY

Answering an inquiry by Rev. Mr. Peronet, the Vicar of Shoreham, Wesley wrote a historic letter now known as "A Plain Account of the People Called Methodists."[2] It has become a significant document for anybody who wishes to understand the early days of Wesley's movement and the practices of his followers.

OPEN SOCIETY

1. Open to all who wished to come.
2. After 2 month probation period eligible for full society membership.
3. Couldn't continue indefinitely.

CLOSED SOCIETY

1. Open to all wishing to "flee from wrath to come."
2. Prescribed rules of conduct.
3. Admission by ticket which could be withheld.
4. Stewards cared for finances.
5. Many activities for members.

CLASS MEETING

1. Originally for collecting money.
2. Focused on behavior of members.
3. Both sexes present.
4. Lay leader questioned each member about spiritual condition.
5. Criticism about leaders lead to training program.
6. Became most influential group in the movement.

TRIAL BAND

1. Function of bands changed as movement developed.
2. Basis of membership to be "justified."
3. Members on trial to determine suitability.
4. Smaller groups than classes 5-7 people.
5. If qualified received tickets.

BAND

1. Purpose "to confess faults one to another."
2. Divided by age, sex, marital status.
3. Leader "modeled role" by first telling his own state.
4. Leader asked other band members "searching questions."
5. Emphasis on "confession" lead to criticism.
6. Members lived by strict rules even covering dress.
7. Special meetings for all the band members.
8. Leaders also met periodically.

SELECT SOCIETY

1. Were inner group seeking "perfection."
2. This was not a static condition.
3. Members motivated development of individual talents.
4. They were to be model for the rest of the society.
5. They had few rules but insisted on confidentiality.
6. The most democratic of all the groups.
7. Wesley himself invited close interaction.
8. These groups soon disappeared from Methodism.

PENITENT BAND

1. For the people who had failed and needed help.
2. Made special application to their individual circumstances.
3. Leader applied "threats" and "promises."

Fig. 1. The steps of group life for eighteenth-century methodist. (Few societies were actually as highly organized as this. It represents the ideal.)

As Wesley tells the story, he and his brother started out with the single-minded intention of preaching the Gospel. While ecclesiastical authorities objected to their enthusiasm, many of the common people heard them and responded to the message. The new converts found themselves in a difficult situation. The churches did not always welcome these "enthusiasts." Many of their former friends were less than cordial, and relatives criticized their religious zeal and warned that much religion would make them mad. Faced with this dilemma, many of these people turned naturally to the Wesley brothers for direction.

John and Charles advised them, "Strengthen one another, talk as often as you can."

The converts quickly replied that they saw the value of this counsel, but they also wanted to talk with the preachers who had led them into their new religious experience. Wesley decided that the appeal of the converts must be answered with some type of pastoral work, so he asked for their names and addresses. As the list lengthened, he saw the impracticality of the program of calling on them he had envisaged; he would never have enough time to visit them all in their homes. So he made the alternative suggestion, "If you will all come together, every Thursday in the evening, I will gladly spend some time with you in prayer, and give you the best advice I can."[3]

So a simple organization came into existence. Wesley describes the process: "Thus arose, without any previous desire on either side, what was afterwards called a society; a very innocent name, and very common in London, for any number of people associating themselves together."[4] Wesley makes it very clear that this movement was completely unplanned and arose spontaneously. He made an analogy between these people and the *catacheumens,* or enquirers of the early church. Because this group involved uniting existing organizations it was sometimes called the United Society.

He quickly noted the benefits that came from this fellowship gathering. The meetings strengthened his converts and encouraged them in their new way of life. He also observed that the people who did not affiliate with the Society soon lost their enthusiasm and lapsed back into their old ways. The conviction continued to grow in Wesley's mind that it was never enough just to preach before a group, call for spiritual responses, and then leave people by themselves. While visiting a town called Tarfield, where the converts from a previous visit had lapsed spiritually, Wesley made a notable resolution: "Therefore I determine, by the grace of God, not to strike one blow in any place where I cannot follow the blow."[5] In practice this meant setting up some type of group into which participants could be initiated.

The subdivision of the Society, called the *Open Society,* existed for those people who looked for an opportunity to continue their search for religious truth in the company of like-minded individuals. Anyone could come and hear the preaching and have fellowship with the society members. However, the merely curious were not allowed to continue indefinitely; a newcomer could only attend for a two-month probationary period before being eliminated or moving into the Closed Society. The *Closed Society* was a meeting for those who desired "to flee from the wrath to come." They had to be genuine seekers.

Wesley also put a plan of action before the Society members—they were to avoid evil, assist other Christians and unite with them in works of charity, attend preaching and communion, and pay attention to private devotions.

Society Leadership Function.   Leaders gave tickets to members of the Closed Society to indicate their good standing. Individuals becoming lax in their attendance were denied a ticket and so eliminated from the closed meetings of the Society. Although members were required to have a desire "to flee from the wrath to come," as a practical matter attendance was the main criterion upon which membership was based.

In the Society the leader reigned supreme; it functioned under his unchallenged control. There was nothing unusual about this gathering; it provided about the same experience as any normal church meeting. The leader used the lecture method as he addressed himself to the group as a whole (Figure 2). He aimed at information and inspiration, and the only interchange was a mental response or an enthusiastic shout from a fervent follower.

Wesley entertained the hope that by association with the members of the Society, some of the religion of the convinced and dedicated might rub off on uncommited attendants. Although it probably seemed to Wesley and his leaders that the important factor was exposure to preaching, in reality the experiences of relationship and affiliation were crucial.

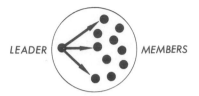

Fig. 2. Society leadership.

THE BEHAVIORAL LEVEL—THE CLASS MEETING

The second level of Methodist group life was the *Class Meeting*, which rapidly became the most influential organization in Methodism. Its uniqueness lay in the way it had evolved from a fund-raising mechanism to a first-line spiritual organization.

The Society in Bristol needed money to pay for the New Room, as they called their meeting place, and in a special conference called to consider the matter, Captain Foy, a sea captain who belonged to the Society, proposed that each member give a penny a week. He then offered to call on eleven other Society members and collect their pennies each week. Several other leaders volunteered to also call on eleven members. While calling on these members the leaders discovered many things about their behavior and reported these to Wesley. Wesley realized that the face-to-face confrontations might be more important than collecting the pennies, and so he suggested that each group meet at the Society's building to discuss their behavior.

Wesley was chagrined when he encountered resistance to what he considered a good idea. The many complaints included, Why should group pressures be used? Shy members will not participate. Why change things? Is it biblical? We don't know why, but we just don't like it.

Such objections have a familiar ring for anybody who has attempted to initiate some type of group program. The same concerns are expressed to this day and represent the fears and apprehensions that surface when the idea of using groups is raised.

The Use of Laity.   The whole idea of Classes brought lay people to the fore, and many of them occupied a humble station in life. In one of his letters Wesley gave lists of band members and their leaders. Richard Leg, leader of band one, was a haberdasher; Henry Crawley, leader of band three, was a barber. Another early list of class leaders names Thomas Middlesborough, a farmer; John Curtiss, a stuff maker; and David Burns, a weaver. Women were sometimes leaders as Grace Murray tells in her memoirs. These people soon became targets for criticism, which was subtle enough for Wesley to pay attention to it. The objection essentially was that the idea was well enough in itself, but the leaders were insufficient for the work. They had neither the gifts nor the graces for such an employment.[6]

Wesley realized he was breaking new ground in this use of lay-people, so he gave a detailed answer to this criticism. He pointed out that despite their lack of ecclesiastical endorsement, God had obviously blessed the work of these laypeople. Some individuals might be inadequate, but he could check on them, and if the accusation proved correct, they could be removed. He added that any members who felt a leader was not capable of doing the job could report the matter to him rather than tattling to others. Wesley assured them he would take appropriate action. He also took pains to remind the class members that he had initiated a "training program." This was a type of in-service training. The leaders worked with their Classes, and each Thursday they met for a session with Wesley himself. He concluded by urging the class members to pray for their leaders.

Leadership in the Class Meeting. The problem of class leadership continued to be a burden to Wesley, and, realizing the significance of this role, he redoubled his efforts to work with class leaders. He came up with a series of ideas:

1. The leaders were to be examined concerning the method they used in their classes.

2. Each leader was to develop a technique of dealing with his class members. He should become a spiritual diagnostician, going beyond the mere observance of outward rules and focusing on the member's spiritual condition.

3. If a leader was not doing well in his class, he was to be transferred to another group; and if he continued to be unsuccessful, he might be removed from his position of leadership.

4. The leaders were to be rotated periodically so that they could meet with other groups of people and learn to work with them.

5. When a particularly gifted leader was noticed, he was to be moved around the classes so that as many as possible might have the benefit of his skills.[7]

This program, with its emphasis on the supervision of the minister
~~and the experiences of the class leader, bears some resemblance to the~~
modern plan of clinical education, in which a trainee counselor works
with a client and, after writing up his experience, discusses his technique with the supervisor who suggests ways in which he or she could
improve. In many of these situations the interaction between supervisor and trainee may be the most valuable aspect of the experience.
The interaction of class leader and minister may have been an anticipation of the clinical education movement.

As the leader functioned within the Class Meeting, his technique
was rather like that of some group leaders who feel they must quiz each
of the group members. The difference would probably be in the focus
of the questions. In the Class Meeting the concern was with the behavior of the class member as each was questioned in turn (Figure 3).
MacKenzie, an English investigator, has noted in his distinction between the Bands and the Class Meeting, "The Classes were concerned
primarily with examining the outward walk while the Bands were more
concerned with inward motives."[8] The leader, very much in charge of
the situation, questioned each member in turn about his or her conduct
during the previous week.

In its composition the Class Meeting was unique. Wesley normally
insisted on the separation of the sexes. In one letter he ordered that
the men and women should sit on separate sides of the meeting place,
threatening that if they sat together he would walk out. But in the
Class Meeting the sexes intermingled in a coeducational system.

The Class Meeting went on to become the most important single
unit in Methodism and was the most durable of all the organizations
set up by Wesley.

THE MOTIVATIONAL LEVEL—THE BAND

The unique gathering of people of all ages and both sexes at the
Class Meetings caused some dissatisfaction. Some people felt they
could not speak openly in such a gathering, so they asked their leader
to provide a setting in which they could "pour out their hearts." To
meet this demand Wesley constituted the *Band*, which was essentially
a peer group of men meeting with men and women with women.

This was the first group that had specific requirements of a spiritual
experience before entrance. Members of this group must be able to

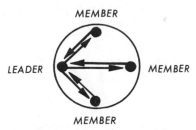

Fig. 3 Class meeting leadership.

claim that they were "justified." They were required to answer a series of questions that gave evidence of their experience of salvation.

In a careful screening candidates were warned of two difficulties they faced in the new group. In the first place, they must be willing to become "open" and confess their failures and shortcomings. A basic aim of the group was to provide a situation where it would be possible to "confess your faults one to another." The second requirement for prospective members was to be able to allow the other members of the Band to tell them of their faults and deficiencies. After this warning the prospective band members entered a Trial Band, in which they spent a period of time before becoming eligible for membership in the Band proper.

The leaders occupied a unique position in the Band. It seems as if in some instances they were selected by the group. The leaders gave the lead to the group by "speaking their own state" first, then leading other members to discuss themselves, their state, and their condition. This technique is used in some types of group therapy and among the modern self-help groups. In Integrity Therapy it is referred to as modeling the role, as the leader always sets the example by admitting his or her own failure before asking every other member to "become open." The leader was to be both a model and a facilitator (Figure 4), setting the example and guiding the processes of interaction between the members of the group.

The idea of becoming open—or confession, as it was popularly known—brought many criticisms. The most vocal of these was that Wesley was perpetuating popery by using a Roman Catholic practice. Another complaint was that such lurid details were revealed that the experience corrupted innocent minds.

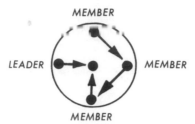

Fig. 4. Band leadership.

Wesley carefully answered every accusation. He began by rejecting auricular confession as practiced by the Catholics, and then pointed out that the Bible taught confession, as did the Church of England. The subject matter of confession might not be nearly as lurid as some people imagined; it frequently had to do with mundane things like pride, self-will, and unbelief. He further indicated that the confession took place not with one person but conjointly with a group, and there were special provisions so that nothing would be repeated outside the group. Lest there be any doubt, Wesley did believe in confession—so much so that his most frequently used scripture verse was probably "Confess your faults one to another" (James 5:16).

A testimony to one of the values of being part of a group in which people are open comes in an eighteenth-century letter by Margaret Austin, who had been attending Methodist meetings but wanted some deeper experiences. She says she had, ". . . a strong desire to get into the Bands. I went to the Rev. Mr. John Wesley and he admitted me. . . . Hearing the others tell the state of their souls was of much strength to me to speak the state of mine."[9] In any group therapy experience this identification process is an important factor, and it played a significant role within the Methodist Bands.

THE ASPIRATIONAL LEVEL—THE SELECT SOCIETY

Even standards as high as those of the Bands failed to challenge some of Wesley's more zealous followers. Perfectionist Wesley realized he needed some type of association that would throw the enthusiasts of a Society into a close relationship with each other. So evolved the groups known as the *Select Societies,* which aimed at perfection—not just a static condition but a state within which the members would continue to strive for this elevated objective.

The Select Societies became the most democratic of all the organizations within Methodism. Though he exercised a tight control over his followers, with these committed groups Wesley made provision for them to join in the decision-making process and air their views about him. The groups were virtually leaderless—the leadership function moved around the group (Figure 5).

Wesley wanted the members to develop their capacities, provoke each other, watch over each other, and interact with him personally. He believed that these people would be a model of what he wanted, so that he would be able to point to them as "a pattern of love of holiness and of good works."[10] The Select Society existed for those extraordinary people who could aspire to Wesley's highest ideals.

THE RECLAMATION LEVEL—THE PENITENT BAND

The rules for each of the groups set out the specific requirements for that particular level. It was one thing to set standards and another for the members of the Society to keep up with them. Wesley was able to exclude the laggards by the simple practice of giving tickets only to those who could meet his requirements for membership in the Society. The steward at the doorway of the meeting refused admittance to those without tickets. Wesley exercised his power reluctantly, but with the awareness that it had to be done.

He was not satisfied merely to exclude people. His pastor's heart told him something must be done to try to restore the drop-outs to their former place. He showed remarkable patience in dealing with them but insisted that they must show a desire to do something. They were drafted into the group known as the *Penitents*.

The Penitents met on Saturday night. Apparently Wesley examined them individually and tried to discover the areas of their failure. In

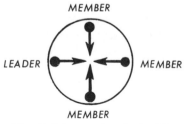

Fig. 5. Select society leadership.

working with them he applied both the "threats" and "promises" of God. According to his record he had good success with many of the penitents, and some of them became outstanding members of the Society.

THE LIFE CYCLE OF THE GROUP

Toward the end of his life, Wesley found himself faced with a different reception from that in his earlier days. Instead of hostile mobs great crowds turned out to bid him an affectionate welcome. The number of his followers increased rapidly, but he feared that although he was gaining large numbers of people, he was losing the spiritual quality he sought.

Wesley pondered the problem of a success that breeds failure, and it seemed to him to be far more dangerous than the opposition and persecution of earlier days. What were the practical steps to be taken to break this vicious cycle? How could "heart religion" be rekindled among a people who were forever cooling off?

The technique Wesley proposed to combat this danger involved using two of the groups he had developed—the Band and the Select Society. He constantly urged the utilization of "Band life and Select Societies." In another notable entry in his journal he instructed his leaders:

To encourage meeting in the Band, (1) Have a love-feast (a gathering where the band members ate a little plain cake and drank water and prayed). (2) Never fail to meet them once a week. (3) Exhort all believers to embrace the advantage (urge society members to join the band). (4) Give a band ticket to none till they have met a quarter on trial (prospective members were to attend for three months before receiving a ticket which indicated they were full members).[11]

While visiting one of the Societies he was chagrined by the neglect of Band life. Just a few days before his death he wrote, "Ye cannot be too diligent in restoring the Bands. No Society will continue lively without them."[12] Wesley's apprehensions were correct; unfortunately they materialized in a later day, as the Bands disappeared.

The great problem of group life is to decide whether a particular group has served its purpose and deserves a decent burial, or if it enshrines within its workings the very spirit that is needed and letting it die will mean the loss of a vital concept. It is disconcerting to find that no sooner have the funeral services been conducted with a fairly decent show of mourning than a new organization comes into existence and gains a great following by using the same principles so recently laid aside as outmoded and old-fashioned.

The church has frequently been oversensitive to criticism about its old-fashioned ideas, and in its modernizing program it has thrown out many of these practices and taken on new types of organization, confident that the outside world will warmly compliment it for keeping up-to-date. It is rather upsetting to discover that not only have the new methods not been particularly successful, but other volunteer nonprofessional groups, such as the self-helpers, and influential systems of psychotherapy, are using very similar methods with tremendous success.

Methodism continued to grow and flourish and is one of the largest and wealthiest church groups in the world today. Some changes have taken place; the Society has become a church; the preacher, a minister. An English magazine recently paid tribute to John Wesley and discussed the way Methodism has gone in recent years. One enlightening comment stated that the number of lay preachers had dropped at an alarming rate.

But even more disturbing for the student of group life is that the units for fostering "heart religion," the Select Society, the Band, and even the Class Meeting have all disappeared.

In a very fine book the authors have tried to reproduce an old-time Class Meeting. There it is, with all its crudities and its extremes; but the reader familiar with group dynamics sees even in this portrayal some very fine practices, as pretense is stripped away, and individual members are given an experience that they would never get in a church today.

A group, like an individual, may have an agonizing struggle to come to birth. After a precarious infancy it grows into a vigorous youth, during which it may make many mistakes and act impulsively, but it functions at the peak of its blossoming, brawny strength. Come middle age, it settles down to enjoy the comforts of its achievements. The settling process continues, often leading to a lingering senility, which may not even be mercifully relieved by a decent death.

THE DISTINCTIVES OF WESLEYAN GROUP LIFE

A number of features of group life became clear from the Wesleyan movement.

1. The Wesleyan groups recognized the importance of individual differences and provided group experience at various levels—association at the Society levels, examination and discussion of behavior at the Class-Meeting level, and self-disclosure at the Band level.

2. Differing patterns of leadership were utilized within the groups. At the Society level leaders addressed the group; in the Class Meeting they questioned the members one at a time; in the band they "modeled" by telling of their own "state," then called for a response from the others. At the Select Society level the group became almost leaderless.

3. The practice of self-disclosure was important. Wesley suffered much criticism because of his commitment to confession, but despite the problems it brought, Wesley continued to insist on the procedure and answered all the complaints with telling arguments.

4. Laypeople gained new importance. High churchman though he was, Wesley gradually gave a larger place to laypeople and used them in his groups. As radical as it must have seemed in his day, he also used women as leaders in his groups.

5. Wesley developed some interesting training programs to prepare leaders for their functions. His programs of supervision have a strangely modern sound.

6. Many of the basic books on group counseling look back to 1905, when J. H. Pratt held classes for his tuberculosis patients, as the starting point for group counseling. But an unbiased observer must conclude that the Wesleyan Band was in many ways a group therapy experience 150 years before the modern practice commenced.

The Wesleyan groups were a monument to John Wesley's superb administrative ability. He showed remarkable insight into group processes by providing such a variety of group experiences. But their disappearance warns us of the difficulties of survival that always face small groups.

IDEAS FOR GROUP FACILITATORS

One of Wesley's favorite ways of teaching was the catechistic method, asking questions. In one of his letters he commended a follower who was teaching children by asking them questions, but in another he pointed out that questions must be carefully prepared and warned against using the Church of England catechism with younger children.

Open-ended questions can be useful in getting a group to move forward. However, both the content and the method of asking them needs careful consideration. You are a facilitator, not a prosecuting attorney. Try not to ask a question that can be answered with *yes* or *no*.

The *six question method* opens possibilities. Gather your group (5-15) into a circle and commence by saying, "We are going to start by asking ourselves some questions." As you ask each question, it is a good idea to set the example by answering yourself first. Then allow each member of the group in turn to answer.

The first question—"State your name, where you lived from 7 to 12 years of age. How many brothers and sisters did you have at this time?"

My own response would be: "My name is John Drakeford. Between 7 and 11 years I lived in Sydney, Australia. I did not have any brothers or sisters; I am an only child. My father left home when I was about 7 years old, so there was just my mother and myself."

The second question—"How did you heat your house at that time?"

My answer would be: "We didn't have very cold winters, but when we did we sat around the wood-burning stove in our kitchen. Sometimes we took pieces from the stove and wrapped them in paper and put them in our beds so that we could keep our feet warm. Once when there was some fire left in the stove fire box, it began to smoke during the night and wakened us with the fear the house was on fire."

The third question—"What room was the center of warmth in your home?"

My answer would be: "I suppose the kitchen. We had a dining room but seldom used it. Most of our meals were eaten around the kitchen table. When we pickled onions or put up fruit we worked around the table."

The fourth question—"Who did you feel closest to in these years?"

My answer would be: "I suppose I was closest to several of my uncles. They would come and visit our home, and I loved to talk with them. I suppose I was hungry for masculine company."

The fifth question—"What was the greatest thing that ever happened to you?"

My answer would be: "I find it very difficult to decide on just one thing, but I suppose it would be that I received my B.A. degree from the University of Sydney. I'd had to struggle hard to gain admission, and it meant a whole new era of life for me."

The sixth question—This one is optional. Judge the climate of your group and see if it is suitable to ask, "What is your biggest mistake in life?" Be prepared again to set the example.

≋ 3. The Oxford Group and Its Most Improbable Offshoot

FRANK BUCHMAN began his career as a Lutheran minister; a native of Pittsburgh, he graduated from the Philadelphia Seminary (Lutheran) in 1902. Although he was earnest and diligent in his work, his interests were such that it soon became clear he would never fit into the pattern of an orthodox parish pastor. His first venture into a different type of ministry came in 1905, when he founded a settlement house for boys. The work prospered spiritually but lacked material resources. As the trustees struggled with the problems of balancing the budget, they instructed Buchman to reduce the amount of money spent on food. In the conflict that followed Buchman resigned with resentment toward the six trustees whom he felt had frustrated his efforts at serving humanity.

Physically and nervously exhausted from the overwork and conflict, Buchman took a trip abroad. While in England he visited the beautiful Keswick lake country and attended a small country church where a woman was speaking about the cross of Christ. As he listened, he became vividly aware of the resentments he had harbored in his heart against the settlement house trustees. Returning to the house where he was staying, Buchman felt he should do something about that strained relationship. He wrote letters to each of the trustees apologizing for his attitude and asking each of them to forgive him.

At supper that evening he recounted this experience to the members of the family. The son of the house, a student at Cambridge University, was impressed with Buchman's story and requested a private

interview. As a result of this conversation, the young man professed
an evangelical conversion to Christianity. The experience at this
significant time in Buchman's life may have set the stage for his idea
of using sharing as a means of witnessing.

From 1909 to 1915 he worked as a YMCA secretary. In 1916 Buchman became a lecturer in personal evangelism at Hartford Seminary
and then launched himself on an entirely new enterprise, known in
its earliest days as the Oxford Group and later as Moral Re-armament.
Essentially a lay movement, it worked first with college students,
gradually widened its basis to appeal to the "up and out," and ulti-
mately moved its emphasis to spectacular publicity and mass methods.

The many facets of Buchman's personality are demonstrated not
only by the remarkable way he gained access to the high society of his
day, but also by his ability to couch his message in folksy, easily understood metaphors. He would exhort his followers, "Don't put the
hay so high the mule can't reach it," and "If a man's got eye-trouble,
it's no use throwing eye-medicine at him from a second storey window." Speaking of a sinner on the brink of changing, "Don't forget
that a hooked fish jumps, kicks, and runs"; and of religion, "It's like
a nice, juicy, thick steak with onions and French fries—you just can't
help but like it."[1]

Walter Houston Clark, who has written at length about the Oxford
Group, says the central assumptions of the early group were:

1. Men are sinners.
2. Men can be changed.
3. Confession is a prerequisite to change.
4. The changed soul has direct access to God.
5. The age of miracles has returned (through changed lives, miraculous
   incidents, etc.)
6. Those who have been changed must change others.[2]

In these early days the group emphasized the "changed life." In
the process the individual passed through a series of steps, which
Buchman alliterated as confidence (which came from speaking truth-
fully to another about one's life); confession; conviction (a sense of
wrong-doing, guilt); conversion (acceptance of an altered way of life);
and continuance (helping others as the individuals themselves had
been helped).[3]

The group established high ethical standards for its members and urged them to aspire to the four absolutes: absolute honesty, absolute purity, absolute unselfishness, and absolute love. These absolutes became the standard for evaluating individual progress. Many orthodox Christians, however, attacked the absolutes as setting an impossible standard of perfection.

Possibly the most important single feature of group life was the practice of confession, for which groupers used the term *sharing*. A technique for personal development as well as a means of spreading the message of the group, sharing not only provided some of the group's most compelling motivations but also became the major target for criticism by the movement's enemies.

The early days of the group's development were characterized by experiences in which groupers stood before audiences to tell about their failures. An observer describes his impressions of a group meeting:

The next meeting of the group, at about eleven o'clock in the morning, was what might be called the crucial point of the conference. All barriers were broken down. Led on by the honest and frank confession of one of the leaders who quietly related his own experience to the group, withholding nothing, telling of a one-time struggle and conflict in his life that had led again and again to defeat, discouragement and at times a morbid despair, this healthy and happy-looking individual told also of the experience in which he had come to see that of himself alone he was inadequate, of his finding God and of the new life that it had meant for him. As he talked, the most convincing factor in his story was his own attractiveness and personality. His radiant countenance and shining eyes, coupled with his winning smile, testified to the truth of what he was saying and many in the group were thinking the same thought as he told his story. The thought was that this man had found something, something real, something that we would go a long way to find.

The group, led by the honesty and sincerity of the man, followed his example and opened wide the doors that lead to a man's inner life. All pretence and hypocrisy faded. For an hour young men and old men saw themselves and others, not only as they would like to be or have others think they were, but as they really were. It was what Frank Buchman would call a "real fellowship of sinners."[4]

Another aspect of confession was what is generally referred to today as *modeling*, called by Buchman *sharing for witness*. In this process group members told about their personal struggles with life, the sins they may have committed in the past, and the way in which they discovered victory over them. It was hoped that in this way the people being approached would see the example of change and embrace the grouper's philosophy.

An example of Buchman's philosophy of sharing for witness is seen in a conversation in which he said:

> You don't know what to do with your sins. I use mine. I drive them like a team of horses. They are my entry into the hearts of other people. Telling them honestly where I have failed often helps them to be honest about themselves. . . . That doesn't mean telling all about yourself all the time, in private or in public. That is wrong. Dead wrong. But you must learn to live free from the pride that is not ready to tell anybody anything about yourself if, in guidance, you see it will help him. Never tell anything to somebody else which involved a third party.[5]

Critics of the Oxford Group zeroed in on the practice of confession. Among college youth particularly, it was inevitable that personal confession should freely mention sex. The whole matter came to a head at Princeton University in 1926, when critics charged, "Buchmanism surreptitiously practiced unwarranted inquisition into personal lives, was dangerous in its handling of sex, and was stimulating a most unhealthy interest in morbid sexual matters among the student body."[6] The accusation was further reinforced when *Time* magazine ran an article noting Buchman's preoccupation with sex.

A special committee at Princeton investigated the charges and concluded there was no evidence to support them:

> It has been charged that in carrying it [i.e., personal work] on, an aggressive form of personal evangelism has been employed which has been offensive to many; that the privacy of the individual has been invaded; that a confession of guilt with particularity has been set up as a condition of Christian life; that various meetings have been held at which mutual confession of intimate sins has been encouraged; that emphasis has been laid upon securing confession of sexual immorality; and that these methods have alienated a large portion of the undergraduate body from affiliation with and participation in the work of the society. . . . We have endeavored in every way to secure any evidence which would tend to substantiate or justify these charges. With the exception of a few cases, which were denied by those implicated, no evidence has been produced before us which substantiates or justifies them.[7]

Another characteristic of the movement was its use of slogans: "The only sane people in an insane world are those guided by God." "Definite direction, accurate information can still come from the mind of God to the mind of man." "Win your argument, lose your man." "Woo, win, warn." These slogans were freely employed in the house parties and other activities of the group.

As the group grew and spread, a subtle change came over both its message and function. It moved from small intimate groups to large gatherings. In 1938 it had taken the name Moral Re-armanent, abbreviated to MRA. Increasingly, it worked with national and world assemblies. A number of the early followers withdrew from the movement, dissatisfied with the shift from individual emphasis to mass methods.

A SURPRISING APPLICATION

Probably nothing surprised Buchman more than the most improbable offshoot of his movement—a new way of dealing with alcoholics and their problems. Buchman himself always had a tendency to fraternize with the affluent and the influential, but it wasn't among them that his principles had their most important and lasting influence. Of all people, a group of alcoholics showed the pragmatic value of Buchman's concepts.

It all began when an alcholic now generally known as Bill W. came into contact with the Oxford Group at the Calvary Episcopal Church in New York, which conducted a mission for alcoholics. Moving to Akron, Ohio, Bill W. found himself struggling with his drinking urge and looked around for some other alcoholic who might be having a similar difficulty. He finally made contact with Dr. Bob, a surgeon who, coincidentally, had also been associated with the Oxford Group.

As these two men talked and shared their experiences, they became aware of the value of fellowship and relationship, and a small group gradually came into existence. Moving from strength to strength and gaining personal control, they felt that from their own experience of victory they could reach out to help others who were struggling with alcoholism. So was born Alcoholics Anonymous.

Growth was slow, but three groups gradually emerged at Akron, New York, and Cleveland. Although there weren't more than forty recoveries among the groups, and despite the slowness of its development, the small organization decided that its members' experiences should be recorded. The book they wrote was called *Alcoholics Anonymous,* and it settled the question of the official title of the organization.

In this volume alcoholics bared their souls to describe how alcoholism looked from the inside, and it included thirty case studies and histories of alcoholics who told about their difficulties with alcoholism and the way they had gained victory over it.

Probably the most important function of the book was to codify the famous twelve steps that are the heart of the Alcoholics Anonymous program. In their final form they read:

1. We admitted we were powerless over alcohol . . . that our lives had become unmanageable.
2. Came to believe that a Power greater than ourselves could restore us to sanity.
3. Made a decision to turn our will and our lives over to the care of God *as we understood Him.*
4. Made a searching and fearless moral inventory of ourselves.
5. Admitted to God, to ourselves, and to another human being the exact nature of our wrongs.
6. Were entirely ready to have God remove all these defects of character.
7. Humbly asked Him to remove our shortcomings.
8. Made a list of all persons we had harmed and became willing to make amends to them all.
9. Made direct amends to such people wherever possible, except when to do so would injure them or others.
10. Continued to take personal inventory and when we were wrong promptly admitted it.
11. Sought through prayer and meditation to improve our conscious contact with God *as we understood Him,* praying only for knowledge of His will for us and the power to carry that out.
12. Having had a spiritual awakening as the result of these Steps, we tried to carry this message to alcoholics and to practice these principles in all our affairs.[8]

With the publication of the Big Book, as it is most generally called, the organization seemed to be galvanized into action, and alcoholics flocked to A.A. by the thousands. From the original beginning of just two men, the movement has expanded until today there are some 14,000 groups, with a total of over 300,000 members in the United States and ninety other countries.

With success and expansion came problems. In one of its publications A.A. described the crises with which it was confronted: "Everywhere there arose threatening questions of membership, money, personal relations, public relations, management of groups, clubs, and scores of other perplexities."[9] Though members may not have realized it, A.A. now passed through its most critical period. As significant as were the Twelve Steps, the organization within which the program was to be carried on was of the utmost importance. It was out of this vast welter of explosive experience that the guidelines known as A.A.'s Twelve Traditions took form; they were first published in 1946 and later confirmed at A.A.'s first international conference held in Cleveland in 1950. *Twelve Steps and Twelve Traditions* (New York: A.A. World Services, 1965) portrays in some detail the experience that finally produced the Twelve Traditions and gave A.A. its present form, substance, and unity. The Twelve Traditions are:

1. Our common welfare should come first; personal recovery depends upon A.A. unity.
2. For our group purpose there is but one ultimate authority—a loving God as He may express Himself in our group conscience. Our leaders are but trusted servants; they do not govern.
3. The only requirement for A.A. membership is a desire to stop drinking.
4. Each group should be autonomous except in matters affecting other groups or A.A. as a whole.
5. Each group has but one primary purpose—to carry its message to the alcoholic who still suffers.
6. An A.A. group ought never endorse, finance, or lend the A.A. name to any related facility or outside enterprise, lest problems of money, property and prestige divert us from our primary purpose.
7. Every A.A. group ought to be fully self-supporting, declining outside contributions.
8. Alcoholics Anonymous should remain forever nonprofessional, but our service centers may employ special workers.
9. A.A., as such, ought never be organized; but we may create service boards or committees directly responsible to those they serve.
10. Alcoholics Anonymous has no opinion on outside issues; hence the A.A. name ought never be drawn into public controversy.
11. Our public relations policy is based on attraction rather than promotion; we need always maintain personal anonymity at the level of press, radio, and films.
12. Anonymity is the spiritual foundation of our traditions, ever reminding us to place principles before personalities.

Some of the principles of Alcoholics Anonymous as an organization that emerge from these traditions are:

1. A deeply religious note pervades all formulations.
2. Each group is autonomous, with its own financial basis and freedom from outside influence.
3. They reject all forms of bureaucracy; leaders are considered trusted servants.
4. The importance of laypeople is stressed through an insistence that the organization be nonprofessional.
5. The necessity of personal motivation—a desire to stop drinking—is the sole qualification for membership.
6. The principle of anonymity permeates all activites.

WIDENING PERSPECTIVES

An issue of the Alcoholics Anonymous magazine *Grapevine* contained an article dealing with money. One married couple had the drinking problem under control but not the family finances. They finally concluded their difficulty was not really financial but rather a defect of character. To deal with their problem, they followed the simple procedure of taking the Twelve Steps and substituting the word *money* for *alcohol.*

Compare their new Twelve Steps with the efforts many churches make to show the relationship between religion and money. The stewardship campaigns with a long softening period, labored biblical applications, and the encouragement of competition between contributors are often worthy of Madison Avenue at its worst. The rationale seems to be to show how God demands that his devotees give a fair proportion of their money to the church, or else. The adapted Twelve Steps have a much more appealing emphasis on personal responsibility, acknowledgment of failure, and preparation of a plan for personal action with God overshadowing all the specifics of finances. The steps transform the religion–money relationship into a moving spiritual experience.

Yet another article in *Grapevine* tells of an application of the Twelve Steps to the problem of smoking. Weaned from his bottle, one alcoholic nevertheless continued to suck on his cigarette, and, becoming aware of the dangers to his health, he decided to do something about it. He made a successful application of the Twelve Steps to his difficulty.

Charles L. Allen, a very popular religious writer, has produced a book of devotional readings, called *Twelve Ways to Solve Your Problem* (Westwood, N.J.: Revell, 1954). It consists of a series of expositions of the Twelve Steps of Alcoholics Anonymous. The twelve sections of the book are:

1. I Admit I Need Help
2. I Believe God Can Help
3. I Decide for God
4. I Look at Myself
5. I Confess Myself
6. I Am Ready to Be Changed
7. I Ask God to Help
8. I Think of Those I Have Harmed
9. I Make Amends
10. I Continue to Look at Myself
11. I Draw Closer to God
12. I Help Others

In his introduction Allen says, "I have learned that the basic solution to all personal problems is pretty much the same. Bill and Dr. Bob worked out a twelve-point Program of Recovery for the alcoholic. These same twelve steps work equally well no matter what the trouble is. These are really basic principles of the Christian faith."

These uses of the Twelve Steps illustrate how new self-help groups periodically develop emphases to meet the crises of human experience. The basic tenets of self-help groups have a wide application. The principles and techniques already successful in one exigency are fairly easily transferred to an altogether different area of human need. The accomplishments of A.A. were so dramatic that Gamblers Anonymous, for instance, merely changed the words of the Twelve Steps so that they applied to gambling.

Members of the Neurotics Anonymous group promise themselves daily, "I will criticise not one bit, and not try to improve anybody except myself." This is about the only original statement of the organization, which fashions everything it does on the model of A.A. The only change of A.A.'s Twelve Steps is to make the first step read, "We admitted we were powerless over our emotions." All the facets of

A.A.—the Twelve Steps, Twelve Traditions, even the diagrammatic curve used to describe the development of alcoholism—have been adapted by Neurotics Anonymous to chart out an interpretation of the process of emotional illness and recovery. Critics zero in on the over-simplified definition of the neurotic as "any person whose emotions interfere with his functioning in any way, and to any degree whatso-ever as recognized by him."[10] But the group claims a recovery rate of seventy percent and has been recognized by the California Department of Mental Hygiene and the Veterans' Administration hospitals.

Other groups, like the Seven Steppers, a self-help group commenced by ex-convict Bill Sands' work with pre- and post-released convicts, have consolidated the Twelve Steps into Seven Steps with an appro-priate emphasis. Integrity Therapy, sometimes called "A.A. in civilian dress," has used a similar theory, applying it to human relationships and emotional turmoil. The early leaders of Synanon, who worked with drug addicts, were members of A.A. using A.A. methods before moving into a more distinctive intensive program.

All such groups have demonstrated the viability of a number of principles that can be applied to almost every area of human exper-ience and all forms of group life. The challenge now may be to exercise our skills to show just how the principles may be applied to yet other areas of human experience.

And the religious impulse continues.

Speaking at the twentieth anniversary meeting of Alcoholics Anony-mous, one of the founders of the organization, Bill W., paid a tribute to Dr. Sam Shoemaker. After referring to the influences of this re-markable minister he said, ". . . the early Alcoholics Anonymous got its ideas of self-examination, acknowledgment of character defects, restitution for harm done and working with others straight from the Oxford Group."

Once again an essentially religious movement provided an impulse, a motivation, and a way of doing things that became very successful in ameliorating the most stubborn human problems. Why are these techniques continually lost to the church? Why does the church turn from methods distinctly religious and readily embrace purely secular theories? It surely is a puzzle. As Winston Churchill said about Russia's intentions at the outbreak of World War II, the attitudes of churches to self-help groups are "a riddle wrapped in a mystery inside an enigma."

IDEAS FOR GROUP FACILITATORS

Alcoholics Anonymous, like the Oxford Group, uses maxims. Here are some sayings you might find helpful in stimulating your group:

We have no perfect people in our group. We have all failed at some point in our lives.

We are all strugglers together in the sea of life.

We acknowledge our own failures before we discuss the weaknesses of others.

We do not confess for others, but we concentrate on our own shortcomings.

A man is never stronger than when he is admitting his weaknesses.

We cannot accept good reasons for bad behavior.

We alone can do it, but we cannot do it alone.

Act as if . . . (A method by which the subject changes his behavior to change his feelings or attitudes). "Act as if you *did* love your wife."

It is much easier to act yourself into a new way of feeling than to feel yourself into a new way of acting.

We can't stop feeling, but we can direct behavior.

Do the thing and the rewards will emerge.

Our good deeds are our psychic assets, while our irresponsible acts are our liabilities.

We have no spectators, only participators.

Don't sit near the fire if your head is made of butter.

You can't help it if the birds fly over your head, but you can stop them from making a nest in your hair.

You didn't get into trouble overnight; you won't get out of it overnight.

Environment may have made you what you are, but you have no excuse to stay that way.

Becoming an open person is like peeling the skin of an onion, one layer at a time.

Do not nurse resentments; throw them out into the winter's night to the death they deserve.

THE SERENITY PRAYER

God grant me the serenity
to accept things I cannot change,
courage to change things I can,
and wisdom to know the difference.

PRINCIPLES

The purpose of Peer Self-Help Psychotherapy Groups is to change people and these amateurs succeed in a considerable number of cases—apparently more often than professionals do. If the methods developed in Peer Self-Help Psychotherapy Groups were to be refined scientifically and fed back into these groups (with their permission and cooperation), they might be even more effective than they are. These methods could then be applied in whatever professional psychotherapy activities may be needed and which would then be as helpful as Peer Self-Help Psychotherapy Groups.

—NATHAN HURVITZ*

*Nathan Hurviz, "Peer Self-Help Psychotherapy Groups and Their Implications for Psychotherapy," in O. Hobart Mowrer and Anthony J. Vattano, et al., *Integrity Groups: The Loss and Recovery of Community* (Urbana, Illinois: Integrity Groups, 1974), p. 152.

≋ 4. The Therapeutic Function of the Group

THE WORD *water* would forever be indelibly imprinted on Helen Keller's mind. She frequently recalled the scene beside the well redolent with honeysuckle in Tuscumbia, Alabama. There, as the cold water flowed over six-year-old Helen's hand, the teacher's hurrying fingers tapped out the letters, *w-a-t-e-r*, and Helen later remembered the way in which the mystery of language was symbolized by the cold something flowing over her hand. She said, "That living word awakened my soul, gave it light, hope, joy, set it free."[1]

Words now had significance. Previously Helen had struggled to learn a meaningless series of letters; now they combined into words representing something. She learned many words that day, just how many she could never recollect, but she remembered, "I do know that mother, father, sister, teacher, were among them—words that were to make the world blossom for me, 'like Aaron's rod with flowers.'"[2]

These words made the world blossom because they were words of relationship. The maximum punishment in a prison is solitary confinement, and the greatest agony of the prisoner in solitary is not so much bread and water as the isolation and separation from other human beings. Relationships will always have to be a focal point when the human personality is under consideration.

TWO APPROACHES

One way of thinking about personality theorists is to divide them into two groups—the intrapsychic and the interpersonal theorizers.

Those of the *intrapsychic* school look within people to see what makes them tick. One of the most widely known of these theories sees three functional areas: the id, ego, and superego. The *id* refers to the unregulated urges, those forces of personality that mainly have to do with sex and aggression. At the other extreme is the *superego,* the value system or conscience. Between the id and the superego stands the *ego,* or the decision-making self. These are the intrapsychic aspects of personality.

The intrapsychic personality theorists speculate that an individual's adjustment to life is determined by the condition of these systems. While the primitive pressures of the id continue with constant vigor, the ego and superego may be underdeveloped or may have grown too rigid and demanding. Once these three systems get out of kilter, the subject may fall into an internal confusion sometimes referred to as neurosis or psychosis.

Operating on this basis, the intrapsychic theorist spends much time trying to discover how the systems got into their present condition, checking out the individual's history of development, searching back into the misty unconscious of the past, and trying to repair the damage to the intrapsychic factors.

Interpersonal theorists, on the other hand, use an entirely different approach, investigating the subject's associations and relationships. They feel that the secret of an individual's adjustment to life lies in his or her relationship with others. These particular students of personality have concluded that altogether too much time has been spent on considering what goes on within an individual and not enough on interpersonal relationships, which may be the real cause of trouble. So has come an interpersonal theory of personality. Harry Stack Sullivan, a leader in this field, defines personality as ". . . the relatively enduring pattern of recurrent interpersonal situations which characterize a human life."[3] This concept immediately introduces the importance of socializing experiences.

All of life is an ongoing, expanding series of relationships in which individuals are constantly coming to terms with the society around them. This society takes many forms, diagrammed in Figure 6. Infants enter life alone, but soon learn of a concerned parent who is there to minister to their every need, so society is first apprehended as benevolent and kind. As self-awareness dawns, the infant discovers a wider circle in the form of other family members. The first conflicts come from the limits placed upon the developing child, who gradually

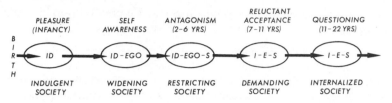

Fig. 6. The individual and society are constantly interacting with each other. The individual's internalized reactions are on the top line of the diagram; his or her perceptions of society are indicated below. In the process, the system's id, ego, and superego are emerging, as indicated on the center line.

apprehends the restrictive nature of society. Childhood brings a society of family, church, and school, all of which lay obligations upon the child; so the child reluctantly accepts a demanding wider society. Adolescence comes with its emotional turmoil, developing interests in wider social groups, and a new intellectual awakening, which may manifest itself in a questioning of previously accepted ideas. At the same time the individual's value system is being further refined. This value system, or conscience, which I define as "the internalized voice of an idealized society" will be the individual's guide into adulthood.

At least partial confirmation of this concept comes from some work done by Canadian investigators. They worked in the fascinating field of studying twins. It had long been known that, in their early years twins, have lower IQs and grasp language more slowly than do non-twins. Using video equipment to observe the home settings of forty-six sets of twins and an equal number of non-twin children the same age (2½ years), they compared and contrasted the two groups. A computer analysis of the way parents and children interacted revealed the twins received shorter hugs and less praise, and were spoken to less frequently than non-twin children. The observers saw this unwitting neglect by parents of twins to have more effect on the intellectual development of twins than did the social or educational background of the parents. They also noted that when one twin dies shortly after birth, the survivor develops verbal skills as quickly as non-twin children. The researchers concluded that parents of twins should spend more time talking to and showing affection toward twins.

The interaction of the individual with society is tied in with the development of both the ego and the superego, as is seen in Nathan

Ackerman's concept of homeodynamics (see Figure 7). From his wide experience in family therapy Ackerman states his position:

Intrapsychic equilibrium cannot be divorced from interpersonal equilibrium; and, at any instant, personality is simultaneously oriented to inner and outer experience. Each direction of orientation continuously influences the other. Stability and growth of the self must be seen as fundamentally tied to stability and growth of interpersonal relations.[4]

If Ackerman's idea is valid, and the evidence mounts to show it is, we may have already defined the pathway of healing the hurt of human beings. It is obviously impossible to reach inside individuals and straighten them out, but it may be possible to manipulate the milieu in which they function if they can be involved in an intensive group experience.

COMPOSITION OF THE GROUP

If the group is so important in the therapeutic process, we must pay attention to its composition. Irvin D. Yalom, Stanford University School of Medicine psychiatrist, has indicated there are two theoretical approaches to this question, and they may be gathered under the headings of heterogeneous group composition and homogeneous group composition. The heterogeneous group composition theories can be further divided into the social microcosm theory and the dissonance theory.[5]

Heterogeneous Group Composition. A group based on the social microcosm theory would be composed of people who in some way are

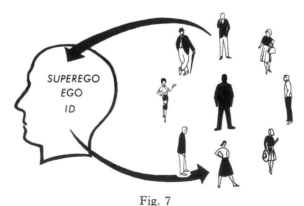

Fig. 7

representative of the real world in which the participants live. This is implied by the very word *microcosm,* literally meaning small world. Ideally such a group would include both men and women, children and older people, from different socioeconomic backgrounds and educational levels.

Obviously it would never be possible to get anything like an exact reflection of the larger society in a small group, but many group workers are satisfied if they can get some diversity among the group members and thus provide a setting for experiences of coming to terms with society.

Proponents of the dissonance theory plan to put participants in a situation where there will be varied elements, with the hope of dissonance and tension in the group. Some of the members will be antagonistic to others, and in this state of discomfort they will strive to reduce the tension by trying new forms of behavior. This dissonant group will frustrate and challenge the participants compelling them to reexamine their attitudes and behavior patterns.

I once participated in such a group. I tried to look nonchalant and unconcerned as I sat in the room with my assigned group. A man led off with a blast of abuse at a Puerto Rican, his superior at work, who had offended him by his attitude and who was sitting opposite him in the group. To say that the statements were candid would be a gross understatement; in a couple of minutes he was pouring out a torrent of abuse, shouting and using language that shocked and amazed my middle-class, seminary-sheltered values. The Puerto Rican, somewhat more under control, responded with vehemence. After a period in which I was afraid that there might be a fight at any moment, the interchange gradually became less offensive, and the emotion subsided, to be followed by a much more rational discussion. Like a forest fire apparently extinguished at one spot but blazing into flame in another, it was only a moment before others in the group were virtually at each others' throats as the focus moved around and allowed prejudices, hostilities, and animosities to be vented. Those two hours were among the most exacting I've ever experienced.

One sponsor, observer, and participant describes one of the differences between this type of encounter and normal group therapy:

Every member is expected to react spontaneously on a visceral level, employing, if he feels the need for it, the crudest terminology and vehement verbal expression. The group concentrates on reaching a "gut level" with the intent of having participants react at a rock-bottom emotional level, rather than on the intellectual plane that is so frequently characteristic of conventional group therapy.[6]

The success of this type of group in working with drug addicts indicates that some positive values emerge from the experience of dissonance, at least in groups working with particularly difficult cases. Whether this technique is advisable in dealing with more "normal" types of groups may be open to question.

Homogeneous Group Composition. The simple understanding of what is sometimes called the *cohesiveness* theory is that attraction to a group lies in being with a number of people who have a similar view of life and comparable interests. The sense of being with individuals facing like problems brings new confidence in facing the difficulty.

Although I have made a distinction between homogeneity and dissonance in types of group functioning, the techniques might not be nearly as different as many imagine. All groups are homogeneous in that they have some common elements; all are heterogeneous because of the members' individual differences in both outlook and expectations.

Yalom points out that though there is no group therapy research evidence for the value of the dissonance theory, there is obvious value in exposing group members to a variety of conflict areas and different styles of coping with problems.[7] However, there is small group research evidence to support the cohesiveness concept. Groups based on some points of similarity rapidly develop cohesiveness, have better attendance, give the participants more freedom, and have a better therapeutic outcome.

THE CASE FOR GROUP THERAPY

In one interesting piece of research an effort was made to discover just what were the most helpful elements of group therapy experience. Using the Q-sort method, people who had been in group therapy were given sixty statements about group therapy reactions and asked to select the ones that most nearly reflected their experiences. The ten items the subjects considered the most significant were:

1. Discovering and accepting previously unknown or unacceptable parts of myself.

2. Being able to say what was bothering me instead of holding it in.

3. Other members' honestly telling me what they think of me.

4. Learning how to express my feelings.

5. The group's teaching me about the type of impression I make on others.

6. Expressing negative and/or positive feelings toward another member.

7. Learning that I must take ultimate responsibility for the way I live my life no matter how much guidance and support I get from others.

8. Learning how I come across to others.

9. Seeing that others could reveal embarassing things and take other risks and benefit from them helped me to do the same.

10. Feeling more trustful of groups and of other people.[8]

This study will provide us with a point of reference, and we will periodically refer to it as the discussion proceeds.

Against this theoretical and experimental background we can better understand the case for group counseling as opposed to individual, one-to-one counseling. We will examine six of the arguments for the superiority of group counseling.

1. Group Counseling Highlights Relationships.   As we have already seen, the whole process of personality development consists of a series of relationships and learning to cope with increasing numbers of people. Society takes different forms over the period of a lifetime. It moves from being indulgent in infancy to restricting in childhood with its "you must," but only when the internalized society gives the individual a sense of "ought" is there a viable adjustment to life and its requirements.

If we accept the idea of the crucial place of relationships in the development of personality and suggest that troubled individuals have removed themselves from relationship and isolated themselves from others, it will follow that therapy should aim at reversing the process. A one-to-one counseling experience provides a starting point, but no more than that. Continued over an indefinite period, it may become a secret shared by two people, but it will still be a secret. The process must proceed further. So the group becomes the means by which the counselee enters into a whole new series of relationships.

Like individual counselors, some groups are good and some not so good. A really good group becomes a microcosm, or small world. In some ways this group of people represents the world within which the difficulty started, and it is therefore a very appropriate environment within which to struggle with the problem.

2. A Good Counseling Group Builds Trust and Confidence.   Not all counselees are enthusiastic about group counseling. Some subjects show great resistance, insisting that their case is peculiar and can be properly dealt with only on an individual basis. This very resistance may actually indicate the area of their greatest need—they have withdrawn and isolated themselves from others. A group constitutes a challenge to this most vulnerable point in their personality. If counselors surrender in the face of this type of resistance, they may deny counselees their best opportunity for help.

Many counselees will maintain, "I cannot talk in the presence of a group; it would be impossible for me to bare my soul before a number of other people." Yet the experience of one counseling center, which functioned on a one-to-one basis for a long period before switching to group practices, has been that people are more open before a group than they were in one-to-one counseling. Many women, particularly, discussed very intimate and personal matters much more freely than they ever did in individual counseling.

Suspicions are gradually allayed. Those who join a group hear about a "covenant of confidentiality" and discover there is no desire to exploit them, only to help. Whereas they formerly looked at every new acquaintance with a questioning eye, they now come to have faith in a group of people who are concerned about them and listen intently whenever they speak. Thus they gradually develop an attitude of trust toward others.

All of this was confirmed in Yalom's study, which showed that among the ten factors that were seen as significant by participants in group therapy was feeling more trustful of groups and other people. This seems to be a common reaction to group situations.

3. Groups Frequently Build Self-Esteem.   In a good group members soon discover they can help someone else. One of the marks of a capable leader is that he or she recognizes that even though counselees may not have their own problem completely under control, they can help someone else, so the leader works to move them into deeper group situations. As group members make their first feeble effort at helping others, they gradually become aware of new abilities. Their self-esteem grows. Life begins to look better. In helping someone else they have helped themselves.

One man who joined a group came in very bad shape. However, once committed to the group he worked diligently and began to show marked improvement. As time passed, he was invited to become a "helper," and he functioned so effectively that he finally became a group leader. In an interview with the director of the counseling center, he was asked what aspect of group therapy had helped him most. He astounded the director when he said, "When I came to that group I was whipped, and in the group I gradually found myself. But the greatest single factor was when you invited me to become a helper. I had a new glow of self-confidence."

Abraham Maslow, a humanistic psychologist, has pointed out that human beings are perpetually wanting animals. They have a series of needs: physical requirements, safety, love, esteem, and self-actualization. What they have the capacity to become they must become. In a group experience they often find this opportunity for self-fulfillment.

4. Group Experiences Provide Feedback. In the process of presenting their problems to the group, counselees encounter a variety of reactions and feedback from the other members. Because of these responses they are able to see their difficulties from a number of different points of view and take a look at them from a new perspective. In Yalom's study of the outcomes of group therapy experience, four of the items (numbers 1, 3, 5, and 8) seen as important by participants concerned feedback.

In some forms of counseling the counselors sees their task as being a mirror—a mirror in which counselees are able to catch a glimpse of themselves as they really are. Mirroring is much more effective when done within the group than during individual counseling. A troubled individual might be reluctant to accept the judgment of one person, even the counselor, but finds it more difficult to reject the consensus of the group. This feedback factor is so important that it will be discussed at length in Chapter 5.

5. Group Counseling Provides Experiences of Interaction. The skillful leader of a group carefully controls the dynamics of the group, bringing them to bear on the members of the group. Isolation is probably the biggest single problem people face today. It is easy for them to listen to such counsel as "You should move toward people," then just give their shoulders a helpless shrug. But within a group the sensitive leader can use the forces of group interaction as an effective influence.

These experience of interaction have many ramifications. Some years ago Dr. Harry Harlow, Professor of Psychology and Director of the Regional Primate Center, did extensive experiments with monkeys and observed the importance of bodily contact between a baby monkey and its mother. Later experiments in this series involved separating the baby monkeys from their mothers and putting them in cages with their peers. The rather startling conclusions were, "Our observations of the three groups of motherless infants raised in close association with one another indicate that opportunity for optimal infant–infant interaction may compensate for lack of mothering."[9]

Peer groups will perform many functions, but one of the most valuable is providing interaction. The way in which the competent leader uses the principles of interaction will be the subject of discussion in Chapter 9. For the present it is enough to note that within the group the way is opened for a great number of experiences of interaction.

6. Group Counseling Increases the Leader's Effectiveness.   In a day when counselors frequently find themselves struggling to meet the demands for their services, group counseling opens the way for a much more effective use of the counselor's time. In the time that would otherwise be given to one person, the counselor can effectively help six to nine people.

Counselors also find help from an unexpected quarter. Experiences in the group become a kind of in-service training, and many of the participants learn the skills of leadership and become assistants to the counselor, greatly facilitating the work of the group.

Psychoanalysts have long claimed that positive transference, in which the client came to love the analyst, was a necessary part of therapy. My personal experience has shown that this situation may be the test of a counselor's maturity. Pastoral counseling, particularly, is strewn with counselors whose effectiveness has been reduced and marriages compromised because of an emotional involvement with a neurotic counselee. Ironically, this separation is sometimes rationalized on the basis that the spouse "didn't continue to grow" along with the counselor. A group moves away from either positive or negative transference as a number of people become the focus of either resentment or affection, and the counselor is spared the experiences that have been the Achilles' heel of the counseling profession.

In July 1977, a man walked out of a house in Spain, shielding his eyes against the glare of the unfamiliar sun. His snow-white hair and alabaster skin bore evidence to many years lived in the cellar of his house. Now 77 years old, el Señor Protasio had once been the socialist mayor of the mountain resort town of Cercedilla. When Generalissimo Francisco Franco's Nationalist forces took over the village, Protasio Montalvo first hid in his house and then dug a cellar, where he stayed for 38 years. He whiled away the time by feeding crumbs to the sparrows and teaching tricks to successive generations of dogs. Asked why he had remained so long in his cellar, he replied, "Only now did I think it was safe." So the socialist who professed a philosophy that was to change the world spent half his life, a period in which some of the greatest social upheavals of all time were taking place, cowering away in a cellar. Participation in group counseling can be compared to Protasio's seclusion—it involves a certain risk, a willingness to interact with others. We must decide whether we want to be safe, feeding sparrows and training dogs, or to take the risks that are part of life, helping to bring changes in others in the arena of a therapeutic group.

IDEAS FOR GROUP FACILITATORS

LIFE IS A BALL OF STRING

Objectives

1. To increase the awareness of the two-way process of communication.
2. To indicate the way in which two or more people are involved in communication.
3. To dramatize the way in which the communication process binds people together.

Materials Needed

A ball of string

Process

The leader of the group explains the three objectives of the game as set out above, and says, "We will discuss the topic. Family members must have an opportunity to express their opinions."

The procedure will be that only the person holding the ball of string can speak. He or she begins talking, and any group member wishing to speak raises a hand. The person holding the ball decides whether to give the ball of string to the other person. As the ball is handed over, the first person retains the end of the string. Whenever the ball is passed, a group member holds the string at that point, so that a pattern of crisscrossing string is built. So the process goes on with the one holding the ball deciding when and to whom to pass the string, thus allowing another person to enter the discussion. The game proceeds for 15 minutes.

After the game is concluded, open a discussion about what happened. You might try the following questions:

1. Did you notice the way the strings connect up members of the group? This is a visualization of a sociogram which is a diagram psychologists use to show the way people have reacted to each other in a group.

2. What does the pattern of the string tell us about our group?

3. How did you feel when you had the ball of string and could decide whom you would let talk?

4. What about the feeling when you wanted to speak and the possessor of the ball wouldn't give it to you?

≋ 5. Feedback—The Core Experience of Group Interaction

AMIDST ALL the discussion of Zen Buddhism, Transcendental Meditation, Risso Kosie-Kai, and various other esoteric oriental methods of dealing with the problems that beset the human personality, it doesn't seem too extraordinary to enter a discussion about group therapy theory and practice and hear a participant mentioning the Johari Window.

THE JOHARI WINDOW

Just in case you imagine this aperture may be the Eastern equivalent of the rose window in a Gothic cathedral, let us note that the word *Johari* comes from the first names of the developers of this concept, Joe Luft and Harry Ingham, and is the unlikely combination of their two first names, Joe and Harry. The Johari Window has become an important teaching instrument among people who work with groups and can be used to give a symbolic representation of some group dynamics.

The Johari Window (Figure 8) has four quadrants or panes. Each of these panes represents some aspect of the way an individual communicates with a group of other people. The top horizontal line represents the individual—what she or he knows and does not know, while the left vertical line indicates the group knowledge and lack of knowledge. Limited as we are with any chart depicting human personality, it is easy to assume that each of these quadrants maintains a constant

THINGS I:

KNOW   DON'T KNOW

THINGS OTHERS: KNOW	A PUBLIC AREA	B BLIND AREA
DON'T KNOW	C SECRET AREA	D UNKNOWN AREA

Fig. 8. The Johari Window.

size and to miss one of the most valuable features of the concept. As Luft says, "A change in any one quadrant will affect all other quadrants." This interaction of the four areas must be in the background of all our considerations of individual panes of the Johari Window.

The Public Area.   The first pane in the Johari Window is (A) the *public area* of personality, that part of life known to both the individual and others in the group. Characteristically, the subject exchanges information about this area of his or her life with other people. A person who wants to give the impression of a sterling character may offer as evidence, "My life is an open book, I've got nothing to hide," and this is probably the best testimony available. A person who lives at this level feels comfortable, can trust other people, and gives the message that others can trust him or her. The objective of much group therapy and communal living experiments is to help the individual extend this public area of personality. Entering a self-help group, the newcomer is frequently met with the question, "Who are you? Tell us about yourself." In many communal living experiments the aim is for the inhabitants to have "all things in common," and this principle applies to all the experiences of life. In their early, vibrant days the Israeli kibbutzim even shared a common shower arrangement for all the members of the community.

A large public area is highly desirable and in much of the literature is spoken of as the *ideal window* (Figure 9). The major problem lies in deciding just how this public area is to be enlarged. The 1976 presidential campaign of Jimmy Carter brought with it a new campaigning style, as the candidate asked people to "trust him" and projected the image of "the boy next door" seeking the highest office the country had to offer. Probably the biggest single sensation of the campaign came when, during an interview with a reporter from *Playboy* magazine, the "born-again" candidate admitted that although he had never been unfaithful to his wife, he had "lusted after" women in his heart. *Playboy* had a windfall, advance publicity was released, and the press played up the statement with great delight.

What was wrong with Jimmy Carter's openness? The basic principle is that self-disclosure should only be made to "significant others." *Playboy*, with its amoral sexual stand, spending a good proportion of its space encouraging men to "lust after" women, represented the antithesis of Carter's moral convictions—thus the way it gloated over its scoop and played it up. An attitude of openness doesn't mean spreading out the details of personal failure to all and sundry. Confession takes place with significant others; different people are significant at different levels, and a therapy group will frequently come to constitute those significant others.

The Blind Area. Blind spots can immeasurably complicate life. Looking into the rearview mirror of my car I have discovered a blind spot—I cannot see one portion of the road behind the vehicle. When, on occasion, I have blundered into a freeway lane unaware of the way I was affecting other motorists, the squeal of brakes or not-so-friendly honk of another car's horn has given me feedback, a message about how my driving is coming across to other people. The response frequently irritated me, but it was necessary for the safety of myself as well as others. Blind spots about our behavior similarly can get us into just as many problem areas in interpersonal relationships.

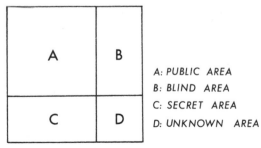

A: PUBLIC AREA
B: BLIND AREA
C: SECRET AREA
D: UNKNOWN AREA

Fig. 9. The Ideal Window.

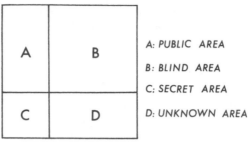

Fig. 10

Pane (B) of the window, the blind area represents the area of which the subject is unaware (Figure 10).

The group should provide the ideal setting within which to reduce the blind area. However, those who need feedback most are not always the most ready to receive it, and they learn to avoid situations in which they can get any feedback about themselves. These individuals may believe attack is the best method of defense, and by constant attack deny the group any opportunity of providing the information they so desperately need.

The Secret Area.   The third quadrant of the Johari Window is pane (C) the *secret area* of human experience, that part of life known only by the subject (Figure 11). When we behave in a way that violates our values, we do it furtively in the hope no one will find out. Writers of literature, whom personality theorist Gordon W. Allport claims might give us more psychological insights about personalities than many academic scholars, have long noted the way secrets affect

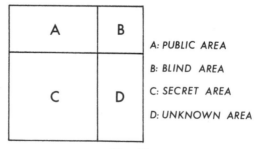

Fig. 11

people. Dr. Ellenberger, a psychiatric historian, has written about such examples from literature and refers to them as pathogenic secrets. Keeping matters secret takes its toll on personality adjustment, alienating the possessor from others and requiring valuable psychic energy to keep the secret concealed.

The Dynamics of Change. Experiences of relationship within groups provide opportunities for bringing changes in the size of the quadrants of the Johari Window. The one technique most readily available to the individual is found in the experience called becoming open, confession, or self-disclosure, which allows individuals to effectively reduce the size of the secret area of their lives. Carl Jung puts it in a clearer perspective when he says, "In keeping the matter private . . . I still continue in my state of isolation. It is only with the help of confession that I am able to throw myself into the arms of humanity freed at last from the burden of moral exile."[1]

Nowhere is the way in which the four panes are related to each other and Luft's principle that "A change in any one quadrant will affect all other quadrants," seen more clearly than in the manner in which a change in pane (C), the secret area, brings a change in the other panes (Figure 12). In a group session individuals are encouraged to talk about themselves in an effort to get at the pathogenic secret and thus reduce the size of the secret area. As the subjects reveal these secrets, not only does the public area enlarge, but the experience of being open encourages other people to provide feedback, and so the blind area is reduced. An outcome not so readily anticipated is the effect on the unknown area. This experience is sometimes referred to by workers with groups as peeling the skin off the onion. Removing

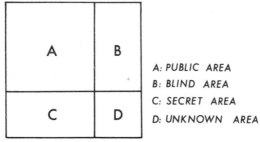

Fig. 12. The Ideal Window.

layers of onion skin causes new layers to appear. Analogously, as individuals talk about themselves, they frequently begin a process of recollecting and recalling hitherto forgotten behavior. Noting the nature of this often sensitive, previously unknown or unrecognized material, an irreverent counselor has commented, "As you peel the skin off the onion, new layers appear, and the more you peel the more it stinks." As new material comes to consciousness, the size of the unknown area is reduced.

The Need for Feedback.   An individual with a large blind area constitutes a special problem. Those who are secretive know within themselves something of what they are hiding, but a person with a large blind area is in blissful ignorance and generally unaware of the situation (Figure 13). One writer calls it the bad breath area. Such behavior generally needs corrective action, but for some reason subjects are unaware of the effect of their behavior on others. It may even be that when they see the same behavior in other people they are dismayed and object to it. If such behavior is ever going to be changed, the subject must have feedback.

A very attractive young lady in one counseling center related her concern about her relationships with men. Because of her good looks and modish dress, she had little trouble in getting a man's attention, and dates came thick and fast; but after a brief, intense experience a man would suddenly lose interest in her. Now in her late twenties, she had high hopes of marriage, and each of these experiences devastated her and left her with a feeling of being exploited. As she told her story, she broke down and cried. When the counselor asked why she did this, she responded in a coquettish manner, "I thought you men like women who broke down and sought a big shoulder to cry

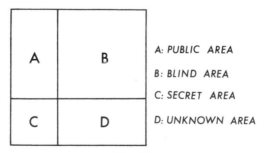

Fig. 13

on." It became clear that she thought this was the way she could make herself more attractive to men. The counselor was able to point out that he was not impressed with her tears; in fact, she came across as a weepy, drooping woman and became an object of pity rather than the attractive person she should have been. She desperately needed the feedback the counselor provided.

Not everybody who needs feedback is willing to accept what she or he is told. Although insensitive to the effects of their behavior on other people, such subjects can become excessively sensitive to information given to them, and respond by becoming angry, crying, threatening to leave, or refusing to talk. The ideal stance in encouraging feedback is to listen; these people may instead become very expressive, believing attack is the best means of defense.

The famous Scottish poet Robert Burns expressed what most of us intuitively know:

> O wad some Power the giftie gie us
> To see oursels as ithers see us!
> It wad frae monie a blunder free us . . .[2]

We all need feedback. But will we get it?

Feedback involves a number of skills. We will consider three of these: the ability to give feedback and to respond appropriately to both negative and positive feedback.

THE PROCESS OF GIVE AND TAKE

The inhabitants of the Oneida community, founded by John Humphrey Noyes in 1848 in Oneida, New York, lived in an unusual relationship in which they practiced a remarkable experiment in eugenics known as *stirpiculture*. By this process they hoped to produce superior children by deciding which couples should be permitted to become parents. The life of the community was so tightly knit that its members shared all their possessions, even to the point of eliminating monogomous marriage commitments in favor of complex marriage, a situation which all the members of the community, at least in theory, belonged to each other.

It is not difficult to imagine the combustible potential of this situation, with people living so close and sharing in such intimate ways.

To cope with this threat, Noyes developed a plan of action called *mutual* or *social criticism,* a technique whereby a member of the community sat in the center of a group and fellow members gathered around and proceeded to tell him or her all the things that needed to be improved.

Charles Nordhoff, a journalist of wide experience, visited the Oneida community and while there attended a mutual criticism meeting. It consisted of a group of fifteen people who occupied benches along the wall of a room. Among the community members sat Noyes, the leader. After the doors closed, a young man named Charles moved to a seat in the middle of the room and made an introductory statement about himself in which he admitted to being aware of a number of failures. The meeting was then thrown open to other community members for their comments about the way Charles came across to them. One at a time the participants told Charles he appeared haughty and supercilious, he was curt, he cultivated the friendship of some people too closely, he was careless in his language even to the point of using slang, his manners at the table were not good, he was too critical and not as humble as he should be.

As Charles sat listening to these statements, his face grew increasingly pale and beads of perspiration appeared on his forehead; but the worst was yet to be. In his role as presiding officer, Noyes made a summary of the criticisms and then dropped his own bomb. The leader told Charles he'd been watching the young man's performance as a member of the community. Charles had fathered a child, and it appeared to Noyes that Charles was losing his sense of community and spending too much time with the mother of his child. Therefore, as the leader he suggested that Charles isolate himself from the woman in question and let another man take his place by her side. Nordhoff goes on to note that Charles reluctantly agreed to follow this course of action, and lets his own personal reaction surface: "Concerning the closing remarks of Noyes, which disclosed a strange and horrible view of morals and duty, I need say nothing."[3]

THE SKILL OF GIVING FEEDBACK

As can be imagined, such a traumatic experience as mutual criticism needed some guidelines, and Noyes provided these in a little book entitled *Mutual Criticism*,[4] gathered under the headings of "Giving Criticism" and "Receiving Criticism."

The instructions to people giving criticism included:

1. The critic must love the person being criticized. In Noyes' graphic language, "Criticism bathed in love wounds but to heal."

2. Criticism must be offered in a spirit of respect for the subject.

3. Criticism must not be undertaken casually or flippantly but seriously and conscientiously.

4. Criticism must be offered from the correct motive, not to allow the critic to vent a grudge against the other person, but to help create a better member of the community.

5. Criticism must be specific, not going around the point but telling exactly what the subject needs to know for self-improvement.

After witnessing a session of criticism, Nordhoff was apparently quite impressed with it. As he wrote about it, he emphasized that the people had apparently been trained to fulfill this function very effectively:

All that I have recited was said by practiced tongues. The people knew very well how to express themselves. There was no vagueness, no uncertainty. Every point was made; every sentence was a hit—a stab, I was going to say, but as the sufferer was a volunteer, I suppose that would be too strong a word."[5]

One of the reasons for the success of criticism in the Oneida Community was clearly the way in which it was offered.

BEING ABLE TO TAKE IT

Most writing on techniques of feedback is geared toward telling the counselor or group leader how to give feedback; very little has been written on how the individual is to receive feedback. Noyes' book included a section that told individuals who received criticism how they should act while other members of the community told them about their faults and failings. The following guidelines were provided:

1. Recipients should maintain a calm, patient spirit.

2. Subjects should look upon this as a test as to whether or not they have an adult or childish spirit. In more modern language, Noyes was

telling his followers that they were mature in terms of the way that they could accept criticism.

3. Subjects were not to be defensive, but were to be willing to "take it" and learn.

4. Silence was the most appropriate response to criticism.

5. The criticism experience was to be looked upon as a many-sided mirror, in which subjects would view themselves.

6. Subjects were warned not to dismiss criticism because the critic might also have similar problems. The experience might make them more adequate helpers.

7. Subjects of social or mutual criticism have a distinct advantage. By their willingness to be criticized by others, they are saved from criticizing themselves.

This list of instructions makes an interesting comparison and contrast with a recent list put out by George Weinberg under the heading of "How to be Criticized":

1. Be quiet while you are being criticized and make clear that you are listening.
2. Look directly at the person talking to you.
3. Under no condition find fault with the person who has just criticized you.
4. Don't create the impression that the other person is destroying your spirit.
5. Don't jest.
6. Don't caricature the complaint.
7. Don't change the subject.
8. Don't imply that your critic has some ulterior, hostile motive.
9. Convey to the other person that you understand his objection.[6]

The members of the Oneida community were so convinced of the virtues of criticism that they offered it to the physically ill members of the community and called the technique *hygenic criticism.* If a community member became ill, the appropriate action was to call some friends to come and offer criticism; it was said to be effective with every illness from colds to diptheria. Noyes' pamphlet on the subject is replete with testimonials from community members to the validity of this technique of healing.

Criticism was seen to be such a valuable technique of community living that, in a burst of enthusiasm, Noyes stated, "We believe that it is only necessary for Free Criticism to be generally known in order to be everywhere appreciated, and to have a shout go up from all true hearts in its favor. For ourselves we shall do all we can to make it popular. Free Criticism is our candidate for the Presidency."[7]

RESPONDING TO POSITIVE FEEDBACK

Many people, curious about the ways of groups, imagine that members spend most of their time attacking each other. In actual fact, the group often focuses upon one of the members in loving care and concern. If one member is manifesting a low self-image, the group may engage in a practice known by such names as strength bombardment, and giving verbal gifts. This technique is in many ways the reverse of what Noyes did with his criticism groups, as each member gives positive feedback, telling subjects something he or she likes about them.

The practice has potential, but unfortunately many people do not know how to respond, and find it much more difficult to accept positive feedback than to accept criticism. Some principles that might help here are:

1. Don't feel compelled to "trade." While it certainly is desirable that you should be ready to return a compliment, to indicate that you are not so self-centered that you do not see something of value in the person who is complimenting you, it is not an absolute necessity. You can accept the compliment in the sincere spirit in which it is offered and say Thank you.

2. Don't deny the statement. There's nothing more devastating than to offer a compliment to someone and have it refused—it's rather like feeding an animal that bites your hand. One group member named Gary Nelson took this attitude. As he sat in group one evening lamenting his lack of ability, he happened to mention he'd bought a stereo kit and put it together. The men in the group all expressed an interest, so the following week Gary turned up with the completed unit in a large box. Harry Gordon, who had a reputation as an experienced radio ham, said, "That's an excellent job, I can see you've put in lots of time in it." Gary replied, "Oh, come on, be honest. It's amateurish and you know it."

Gary embarrassed Harry, who was trying to encourage a newcomer to the field in which he himself had some expertise. How could Gary have responded? One possibility is, "I appreciate a compliment from an expert like you. You encourage me."

3. Look upon positive feedback as a gesture of goodwill and respond accordingly. The old-fashioned meanings of the word *compliment* were (1) a gift, and (2) a present that someone gives to an inferior. Many of us feel it demeans us when someone gives something to us, much the same way as a servant might feel about a gratuity. Take a sensible view of yourself. Don't underrate yourself; you have certain gifts and because of them you are entitled to appropriate appreciation.

4. Don't question the motives of the person who gives you positive feedback. In the sort of competitive society we live in, we are all too used to people softening us up before trying to get something from us. From personal experience I know that when someone compliments me, especially effusively, I wonder if there is an ulterior motive. Am I being set up for a sale? But it may be a person of goodwill who is sincerely trying to encourage me in something I am undertaking, and I should accept the compliment at face value and not have the suspicion that I am being tricked.

5. Don't let the fear of criticism deny you the right to positive feedback. We have all had contact with people who pave the way for criticism by complimenting: "This is very good, but. . . ." So when we hear a compliment we may steel ourselves. But the person giving us positive feedback may have had no intention at all of being critical. Don't rush out to meet criticism halfway.

6. Don't be too naive. Some people like to give a compliment. A young woman in one of my classes would come up after every class with a beaming smile and excitedly exclaim, "Oh, that was so wonderful. Your lectures are so marvelous." I hope they *were* marvelous to her, but I'm realistic enough to know my utterances aren't always inspired; in fact, some of them are very mediocre. Referring to applause, Robert Montgomery once said, "Enjoy it, but never quite believe it." Make a realistic evaluation of yourself.

OUR NEED FOR FEEDBACK

In the course of a varied career in using communications media, I have gradually learned that the way I think I'm getting my ideas across and the way they actually come over to my audience are two different matters. It started with radio. As I sat listening to my first delayed broadcast I said to my wife, "Reassure me, honey; there's something wrong. I don't normally sound like that, do I?" To my chagrin she replied, "It's just exactly you."

Later came television. I had been invited to join a group of educators on a regular weekly panel program. We worked hard at preparing what we hoped would be a model for the programs to follow. This series of conferences led to preparation of scripts and teaching aids, with long discussions of the most effective way of getting our ideas across. After many falterings the program was finally videotaped. Following the taping, the program director took us to a room where the technicians played back our program for us. As we watched what was going to be beamed into the homes of the viewers, it became a moment of truth—humiliating truth for me—as with sinking stomach I watched the way I appeared on that wretched video tube. I journeyed home that night with the conviction that I was a complete flop as a television performer and needed to rethink my whole television technique.

The director responsible for the program had taught us a valuable lesson without saying a single word. As we were able to see ourselves and the way that we came across to other people, we learned in a hurry. Feedback is always an important part of a teaching process.

Feedback is a major function of group interaction. There is a sense in which the members of a group have entered a hall of mirrors and gradually come to see a wide variety of self-images. They may consider some of them disturbing, but at least they have seen them. One basic principle has emerged from many behavioral studies: The more knowledge of results we receive about our performance, the greater is our learning. Among group workers who strive to change other people, one statement stands supreme: "Feedback is the core experience."

> A centipede may be perfectly happy without awareness,
> but after all, he restricts himself to crawling under rocks.
>
> —JOSEPH LUFT

IDEAS FOR GROUP FACILITATORS

Giving feedback is undoubtedly important, but it must be done carefully. Listed below are a series of principles for evaluating feed-

back. Go back over one of your sessions and rate your group on
the following scales:

1. Good feedback is in behavioral terms rather than in generalized
   statements.

   In our group feedback was:

In behavioral						*In generalized*
terms	*1*	*2*	*3*	*4*	*5*	*statements*

2. Effective feedback concerns behavior that can be changed.

   In our group feedback was:

Directed toward						*Directed toward*
changeable	*1*	*2*	*3*	*4*	*5*	*nonchangeable*
behavior						*behavior*

3. Feedback likely to be implemented is sought rather than
   imposed.

   In our group feedback was:

Sought	*1*	*2*	*3*	*4*	*5*	*Imposed*

4. Good feedback is given immediately following the focal behavior.

   In our group feedback was given:

Immediately	*1*	*2*	*3*	*4*	*5*	*Later*

5. The best feedback is a consensus of the group.

   In our group feedback came from:

A consensus	*1*	*2*	*3*	*4*	*5*	*One individual*

6. The recipient of feedback should respond appropriately.

   In our group the recipient's response was:

Appropriate	*1*	*2*	*3*	*4*	*5*	*Inappropriate*

6. Principles of the Peer Mutual Self-Help Psychotherapy Group

I DON'T know what happened to me in this two-year period of my life, but I found myself neglecting my wife, family, and friends, and spending increasingly larger periods of time with the strangest people you could imagine. I consorted with convicts, alcoholics, drug addicts, sex perverts, notoriously obese individuals, and many who might at any moment be picked up and committed to mental hospitals. And I enjoyed every moment of it.

I was on the track of the secret of the peer mutual self-help psychotherapy groups, trying to find out why they had succeeded with people about whom many social scientists were very pessimistic indeed. As Nathan Hurvitz states, ". . . it is likely that more people have been and are being helped by peer self-help psychotherapy groups than have been and are being helped by all types of professionally trained psychotherapists combined, with far less theorizing, analyzing, or pilpuling, and for much less money."[1]

My study was undertaken in an effort to discover some of the principles so effectively used by these rapidly proliferating peer mutual self-help groups. One directory lists nearly three hundred of them; to investigate and evaluate them all would be an almost impossible undertaking. The list itself may be rather misleading, for a closer examination showed that many of the organizations conducted formal meetings with speakers in much the same manner as a P.T.A. or civic club. This meant that my first task was to choose the groups really worthy of the name peer mutual self-help.[2]

The preliminary inquiry used arbitrary criteria for qualifying eligible groups. The term *peer mutual self-help* was applied to a group that emphasized the following:

1. *Responsibility.* The group does not provide easy excuses for poor behavior but insists that individuals accept responsibility for all their actions. This may be the most important single factor in identifying a peer mutual self-help group.

2. *Standards.* A peer mutual self-help group generally has high standards, lays some specific requirements upon its members, and periodically checks on their progress.

3. *Confession.* Provision is made for some form of confession or admission of failure to at least the committed group.

4. *Lay leadership.* The groups utilize laypeople rather than professionals and may even have a suspicion of professionals in their field.

5. *Action.* A peer mutual self-help group focuses on the conduct of its individual members, helping them to evaluate their achievements in a particular area and formulate plans for new types of behavior.

With these critieria as a guide, I examined the available literature and wrote letters to the organizations. The elimination process moved rapidly. Some groups are apparently short-lived, as evidenced by the return of the unopened inquiring letter marked "return to sender." Inadequate secretarial help is probably symptomatic of groups suspicious of professionalism and may have been the reason for some of the unanswered letters. Some of the listed organizations proved to be single individual enterprises that did not have a very wide or long experience. Others showed by a description of their activities that their organization did not really qualify as a peer mutual self-help group.

Since it would have been impossible to investigate in detail all the qualifying groups, I used a sampling technique and chose eight groups for further study. They were TOPS (Take Off Pounds Sensibly), working on weight reduction; Recovery, Incorporated, helping ex-mental hospital patients and nervous people; Yokefellows, a religious fellowship; Alcoholics Anonymous; Seven Steppers, focusing on pre- and postrelease convicts; Daytop Lodge and Synanon, rehabilitating drug addicts; and Integrity Therapy. After selecting these groups, I studied their literature and then paid a personal visit to most of them to try to observe if their practice squared with their theory. My observations are the basis for the information contained in this chapter.

The selected groups represent a wide variety of positions on the spectrum of peer mutual self-help activities. Yet despite the differences apparent in these groups, there are a number of principles common to most of them: socialization, responsibility, high standards, slogans and eipgrams, lay leadership, confession, activity, and modeling. We will examine each of these principles in turn.

PRINCIPLE 1: SOCIALIZATION

There are no wallflowers in peer mutual self-help groups. Whether they like it or not, newcomers are thrust into contact with other people. A sponsor or "buddy" persistently calls to remind them of available help. Joining the group is an act of commitment to an association with others. In the constant round of meetings, classes, and conferences, newcomers learn that they need never be lonely again.

The principle of socialization is particularly obvious in the peer mutual self-help groups working with drug addicts. I have worked with addicts in a clinical setting and noted the way they stick by the "code of the streets." In one group a member looked me in the eye, and then making a gesture that grouped me with the chaplain, said, "It's us against you." Sitting through hours of these discussions, I was frequently frustrated by the total unreality of the atmosphere. The group members were totally conscious that they must stick together against anyone who represented authority.

In the peer mutual self-help groups working with addicts, the code of the streets is completely rejected, and a member of the community is expected to report any violation of rules by a fellow member. At Daytop Lodge a crisis came when one man gave another a pack of cigarettes and then admonished him, "Don't tell anyone I gave them to you." At this moment a staff member entered the room and heard the remark. In the encounter that followed, the group explored the implications of these two men's having a secret from the others.

A similar attitude is seen in the experience of an addict who came to Synanon from the East Coast. He had a history of violence, and his parents insisted that he move to the West Coast and try to start life anew. He did not take too readily to Synanon but had nowhere else to go.

Frankie learned the hard way that the norms of Synanon society are the reverse of the criminal code. On one occasion, Frankie, with two other members of Synanon, went for a walk into town. One individual suggested buying a bottle of wine. (Of course, no drinking is permitted.) Frankie and the other member rejected the proposal. However, no one revealed the incident until two days later, when it came up in a synanon [group gathering]. The group jumped hardest on Frankie and the other individual who had vetoed the idea, rather than on the one who had suggested buying the wine. Frankie and the other "witnesses" were expected to report such "slips" immediately, since the group's life depended on keeping one another "straight." For the first time in his life, Frankie was censured for not telling. The maxim "thou shalt not squeal," basic to the existence of the usual underworld criminal culture, was reversed at Synanon and was ferociously upheld.[3]

Like Daytop, Synanon has no place for the "we–they" dichotomy so frequently found in criminal circles. Adequate socialization experience in this setting demands there be no cliques or "in-groups" and "out-groups"; all the members must be for each other.

But this support in no way lets group members off the hook. The paradox of personal responsibility and group support is summed up in the slogan: "We alone can do it, but we cannot do it alone." New members are told over and over again that the only hope of licking their problem lies in accepting responsibility and relinquishing isolation in favor of close association with others.

PRINCIPLE 2: RESPONSIBILITY

Although a group like A.A. has been diligent in promoting the idea that alcoholism is an illness, the whole thrust of its program points toward an interpretation of sickness that is far different from the generally accepted understanding of the word. It is a sickness in the sense that alcohol is poison to alcoholics; therefore they must stay away from it. This does not mean alcoholics are just helpless pawns, held in alcohol's relentless and unshakable grip. They can and must do something about their state—the peer mutual self-helpers insist that prospective members commit themselves to a life of responsibility.

The principle of responsibility is particularly clear among those groups working with drug addicts. One group insists that addicts come of their own free will, and in the course of an interview will accept no reason for using dope but "stupidity." The director of Gateway House (a group similar to Synanon using the principles of honesty, openness, and responsibility) describes the way an addict is admitted to the facility: "No one is admitted until he's gone through a tough, emotionally bruising interview. He's forced to look at the miserable condition of his life and face the unhappy truth that *he caused it himself.* He learns to *quit blaming* others and start behaving himself as an adult."[4] The director goes on to add that the foundations of Gateway House's program are honesty, openness, and responsibility.

Even such a mundane problem as obesity is attacked through responsibility. Rationalizations abound. Overactive glands or metabolism out of gear are common alibis. Pills are available to control the appetite and elevate the dieter's spirits. But TOPS, a self-help group, instead of relying on medication, summons its members to the hard discipline of a weight-level goal and a plan that may call for stopping eating while still hungry, chewing ice, taping up the cookie jar. When company comes, TOPS members may have to sit at a solitary table, eating off a small plate. They may have their walls decorated with warnings of the dangers of overweight, and even in the seclusion of their room they may be haunted by the sight of clothes three sizes smaller than they now wear, hung there to taunt them to stay on the diet.

Gordon Allport has called attention to the tendency of psychologists to give inadequate consideration to the power of the human will. He says it is possible to look through hundreds of American books on psychology without finding any mention of the words *freedom* and *will.* Human reaction is seen as passively responsive to the inner and outer forces that impinge upon it.

The peer mutual self-helpers totally reject this point of view. Because they see self-decision making as playing a vital role in adjustment to life, the beginning point of the healing experience lies in an acceptance of personal responsibility.

PRINCIPLE 3: HIGH STANDARDS

In contrast to many modern schemes of therapy that are so permissive in their attitudes toward the client, the peer mutual self-helpers set high standards for their members and make heavy demands upon them. It may seem that religious backgrounds spawned these seemingly harsh standards, but Synanon, for example, which has absolutely no religious association, has discovered the value of high standards. Lewis Yablonsky comments:

In the larger society, expense account cheating, kickbacks, and "taking a little off the top" are "standard operating procedures." At Synanon, any indication of this kind of unethical behavior or corruption, at any level, is smashed. Chuck (Charles Dederich, Synanon founder) believes that on an emotional gut level, there is little difference between stealing a tube of shaving creme or a thousand dollars. It appears necessary for the Synanist to swing completely to the "honest side" in order to survive. If he doesn't maintain this complete purity, he may fall, go back to drugs, and pull others with him. His total denouncement of bad behavior becomes an integral part of his own "treatment."[5]

Synanon's high standards have become a point of criticism for some of the orthodox psychological observers of Synanon's program.

When issues of standards of morality are raised, many voices protest the damage of guilt in human experience. The greatest problem in psychotherapy, however, is not the guilt-ridden person; such people can be helped. Probably the most frustrating of all problem personalities is the sociopath. In fact, the difficulty is caused by the sociopath's apparent inability to experience guilt. Without a firm set of values, these individuals are denied the friendly, persuasive voice of conscience helping to make them into the people they really should be.

TOPS doesn't hesitate to raise the individual's guilt level. They have listed the five deadly sins of obesity:

First Sin—Failure to preserve in its pristine glory one shapely body now disfigured almost beyond recognition by bulges and billows displeasing to the eye and calculated to arouse the derision and scorn of the passerby.

Second Sin—Failure to hold the blessings of original comfort, thence to walk in pain amid much puffing, accused of wanton laziness and goaded all the while by numerous and diverse aches, pains, rashes and sundry other matters irritating to both the body and the soul.

Third Sin—Failure to walk with grace and in safety, perchance to falter and topple upon easy provocation, meanwhile finding all tasks difficult and the day's work a tiring ordeal.

Fourth Sin—Failure to protect the body from needless vulnerability to diseases and other maladies, thereby inviting the inroads of heart trouble, diabetes, high blood pressure, cancer, apoplexy, and multiplying the dangers attendant upon childbirth and surgery.

Fifth Sin—Failure to note the shadow of death creeping forward with the addition of each bulge of flesh.[6]

Reminders of guilt appear not only in the deadly sins but also in the processes for weighing in, the fines for failing to count calories, the penalties for gaining, the gentle ridicule of being a pig, the raillery of songs of derision, the warning that "nobody loves a fat girl." Guilt is seen as the goad that will help many people to regain their composure and self-respect.

PRINCIPLE 4: SLOGANS AND EPIGRAMS

Every peer mutual self-help group seems to have its own slogans or eipgrams, and at any meeting of the group they will be heard frequently. Many of these sayings are interchangeable, and one is likely to hear the same catch statement repeated by members of two entirely different groups.

Meeting places of Alcoholics Anonymous are adorned with sayings to give members easy guidelines for decision making. "Easy does it." "A day at a time." "But for the grace of God . . ." "Think, think, think." reminding them of the technique: "We carry the message, not the alcoholic." The Twelve Steps and the Twelve Traditions have become inspired words, giving an easily remembered philosophy for A.A. groups all over the world. Possibly most outstanding the famous Serenity Prayer, "God grant me the serenity to accept the things I cannot change, the courage to change the things I can, and wisdom to know the difference." Although the prayer was not composed for A.A., the group has used it so widely that many people associate it with that movement.

Recovery, Inc., has developed what is probably the most esoteric language of all, including such terms as *outer environment, inner environment, crossover, averageness, sabotage, group-mindedness, symbolic victory*. The main difference between lingo, as Dr. Abraham Lowe, the founder of Recovery, calls it, and the slogans of other self-help groups is that, while most of the other groups' slogans and epigrams make sense and can be used in other contexts, Recovery language is a mystery, something like the verbalizations of a secret society.

Songs have a unique power to penetrate and stick; thus music often has been called into service by the influencers of the masses. Among the peer mutual self-help groups, TOPS is unique in its use of songs to get its message across. One example of these is:

Grow Little Fat Girl
(Tune: "Glow Worm")

Grow little fat girl, thinner, thinner—
Go without your daily dinner,
Eat green salads every day,
That will drive some fat away.
My arm is long, but it won't go round you,
Gee, you're a peach and I'm glad I found you,
But round your waist my arm won't go
Until you thinner grow.

TOPS groups have a whole album of such songs, which help to keep spirits up, while warning of the grave danger of being overweight, and to motivate change.

The Seven Steppers have their own adaptation of A.A.'s Twelve Steps. Their series of statements form an acrostic on the word *Freedom:*

1. **F** acing the truth about ourselves and the world around us, we decided we needed to change.
2. **R** ealizing that there is a Power from which we can gain strength, we have decided to use that Power.
3. **E** valuating ourselves by taking an honest self-appraisal, we examined both our strengths and our weaknesses.
4. **E** ndeavoring to help ourselves overcome our weaknesses, we enlisted the aid of that Power.
5. **D** eciding that our freedom is worth more than our resentments, we are using that Power to help us free ourselves from these resentments.
6. **O** bserving that daily progress is necessary, we set an attainable goal toward which we could work each day.
7. **M** aintaining our own freedom, we pledge ourselves to help others as we have been helped.[7]

Integrity Therapy has a list of slogans adapted from a number of sources to fit many of the particular situations that arise. To emphasize action: "It is much easier to act yourself into a new way of feeling than to feel yourself into a new way of acting." Regarding confession: "We do not confess for somebody else." Concerning the fellowship of the group: "We are all strugglers together in the sea of life." On the power of the group: "We alone can do it, but we cannot do it alone." On putting oneself in a dangerous position: "Don't sit near the fire if your head is made of butter."

The summary of an idea into a catchy phrase gives the group member a little piece of truth to easily grasp and tuck away in a mental recess, close at hand and ready to be used in the moment of need.

PRINCIPLE 5: LAY LEADERSHIP

Whatever happened to doctors' house calls? The general practitioners who periodically visit the home and personally know all the members of a family are a vanishing race. They have given way to the highly trained specialist, living an aloof existence in a well-equipped office, approachable only by appointment and with the payment of a solid fee. It is typical of the era of professional specialization.

Peer mutual self-help groups may be a revolt against professionalism and an affirmation of the value of the common people. Lay leadership is probably the most noteworthy and universal single feature of the peer mutual self-helpers; it is their common denominator.

Lest I give the wrong impression, let me note that emergence of lay leadership is no mere gesture of hostility toward professionalism. The motivation runs deeper than that. Recovery, Inc., launched by a psychiatrist, is very respectful toward psychiatry, urging its members to pay particular attention to their professional therapists. Nevertheless, there came a time when the founder, Dr. Abraham Lowe, concluded that lay people could bring a unique strength to the movement, and he relinquished all control to lay people. One dogmatic rule of Recovery is "The leaders are all lay people. Physicians, psychologists, and clergymen may not become Recovery leaders." Lay leaders were introduced in the best interests of the patients.

And these lay people of the peer mutual self-help groups have developed a remarkable ability to ameliorate the problems of group members. Alcoholics have shown a stubborn resistance to efforts at rehabilitation, and professionals' work with them was far from encouraging. Then a salesman and a physician launched A.A, and as the movement succeeded it became obvious that lay workers brought a distinctive dynamism to their efforts. When the Twelve Traditions were adopted, one of them was, "Alcohlics Anonymous should remain forever nonprofessional."

The situation is similar with Daytop Lodge and Synanon. Drug addicts have long been the despair of professionals, many of whom have worked with devotion at their thankless task. Playing the game by ear and in the light of personal experience, the lay people in these groups have achieved a noteworthy record by using nonchemical and often psychologically unorthodox methods.

Integrity Therapy, founded by a professional psychologist, uses a number of interested professionals in an advisory and voluntary capacity. However, leadership of many of the groups is mixed with lay men and women prominent in the activities. In staff conferences the lay leaders participate on an equal basis with the professionals. The strength of many of these lay leaders is that they have worked their way up—they came originally as members seeking help. Having been through it all, they can now relate with understanding to the troubled group members.

Society has a large stake in the rehabilitation of exconvicts. Many dedicated professionals have labored long and hard at this difficult task with somewhat less than encouraging results. By contrast, the Seven Steppers appear to be chalking up a fine record. The leaders are lay people, all exconvicts. Other interested lay people who have never been in a penitentiary are referred to as square johns and play a subsidiary but important part in the process. Significantly, when I spoke at a Seven Steppers meeting, I was told I was the first psychologist ever to address their gathering.

Most peer mutual self-help groups welcome the interest of professionals. They like to think of them as friends, but they jealously guard their lay leadership. The evidence all indicates they have good reason to be proud of the accomplishments of their lay leaders.

PRINCIPLE 6: CONFESSION

In one of his picturesque phrases, Carl Jung refers to "the burden of moral exile"—the state into which people fall when they realize they have alienated themselves from others. The burden is finally dropped only when they are able to become open and transparent and so return to community.

As part of the emphasis on personal responsibility, and as a means of reintegration into the community, all the peer mutual self-helpers use some form of confession. They insist that members acknowledge their failures as a preliminary to accepting group help.

Not all self-helpers agree on the exact method of confession. The method of TOPS is probably the most elementary of all because the shortcomings of a TOPS member are obvious to all the world. They carry in their bodies the evidence of their dereliction. It becomes a subject of joking and fun before group members, but behind the facade of humor is the acknowledgment of failure.

Some groups use confrontation techniques, by which members tell another person in the group of his or her faults and failures. Yoke-fellow's literature gives illustrations of participants telling fellow members just how they feel about them. This confrontation approach is also seen in Daytop's use of the word *encounter* to describe one type of group meeting. Still other groups are insistent that individuals must confess for themselves; people must confess their own faults before they ever try to make others confess.

Confession is viewed by peer mutual self-help groups as their strength but by their critics as their weakness. Any group with a program emphasizing confession provides certain members of the community at large with an opportunity to circulate lurid stories about their extravagances. The Methodist class meeting, though it had many safeguards, became the target of such criticisms. Later, the Oxford Group was similarly accused; significantly, the criticism focused on the group's discussion of sex.

One of the Oxford Group's problems was the open nature of their meetings. In an effort to prevent such difficulties, Alcoholics Anonymous adapted the technique of maintaining anonymity. The A.A. member commences every presentation with the statement, "I am an alcoholic," but this is generally done in a closed meeting where all the hearers are also alcoholics. Integrity Therapy has anticipated problems by having as one of its guidelines that we only confess our failures to "significant others." We never tell anybody else's story, but we do tell our own story.

Self-disclosure or confession stands at the heart of the self-help groups. A member of a drug group tells of his experience:

Honesty is stressed here, because we are all big liars, very dishonest. It's very hard for people to learn to be honest. There's a fear within us about telling the truth in a situation that might make us look bad. And that's not really necessary here. It's gotten to a point now that if I tell someone a lie I have to go back to him and tell him I lied. I really feel guilty. I have to back off and say, "Hey, it didn't exactly go like that, this is what happened." This all came from people stressing honesty to me.[8]

Confession, so frequently interpreted as an indication of an individual's separateness from society's norms, may in actual fact be a final assertion of solidarity with humanity. People are alike in no one factor more than moral failure. Those who confess drop their pretense and declare themselves at one with the failures of the world. This innumerable company, inwardly awed though outwardly stolid, await the return of the individual. In William James' words, "For him who confesses, shams are over and realities have begun; he has exteriorized his rottenness. If he has not actually got rid of it, he at least no longer smears it over with a hypocritical show of virtue—he lives at least upon a basis of veracity."[9] For many people the peer mutual self-help group provides the only real opportunity for a valid confessional experience.

PRINCIPLE 7: ACTIVITY

Life is one long rush in a peer mutual self-help group. When A.A. say "Take it easy," it doesn't mean sit still, for it is going to run alcoholics off their feet. In some groups life is a constant hectic round of meetings, classes, and conferences. It sometimes seems as if they are determined to fill up every waking moment of the member's life with so much activity that there won't be time to get into trouble.

One of the characteristic sayings of the peer mutual self-helpers is "Act as if . . ." which is possibly an earlier version of the power of positive thinking. If a woman says she doesn't love her husband, she is told to "act as if" she did; it may be that with practice her affection will grow.

Synanon's use of this technique is seen in the talk given to new arrivals:

Here we will teach you how to get the things you want constructively. If you admit that you don't know too much about life—because not knowing got you here, and there has been a lot of psychic pain and nonsense and trouble in your background that you would rather not experience again—then you might accept this intellectually. Don't believe it, accept it intellectually. Say to yourself, "I'm going to act as if he knows what he's talking about."[10]

Yablonsky comments, "For Synanists the first step towards becoming 'clean' is to 'act as if. . . .'"[11]

Some newcomers are quick to claim that this is a deceptive practice. They were earlier warned against deception, and now "act as if" seems as if they are being told the opposite. The answer generally given is that such activity is good or bad according to the motivation. If a person pretends in order to gain a selfish end, it is deception and wrong. If it is part of a plan of disciplined activity in an effort to bring about an internal change, it is "acting as if" and commendable.

Integrity Therapy's statement is, "It is much easier to act yourself into a new way of feeling than to feel yourself into a new way of acting." Synanon says, "We can't stop feeling, but we can direct behavior," and "Do the thing and the rewards will emerge." Yablonsky notes that Synanon has even anticipated the Ackerman concept of homeodynamics by stating that positive behavior will influence the intrapsychic processes.

Recovery's exhortation, "Move your muscles," has a similar implication. Recovery's Dr. Lowe makes the most advanced claim for an activity technique when he says that the muscles are frequently the teachers and educators of the brain.

A.A. members are hard at work on their Twelve Step work, which means they are out carrying the message to other alcoholics. TOPS members check up on their "buddies." Integrity Therapy members with their symptoms under control lead a group.

Such activity is not just altruistic. Members of a peer mutual self-help group learn that the only way they can become successfully functioning personalities is to commit themselves to helping others. As Synanon puts it:

The Synanist has a strong personal involvement with straightening out his fellows. He begins to understand that it is for his own enlightened self-interest and benefit. If another person is helped it also helps him since the other is part of the same community. Attacking the "mask of crime" and resocializing his fellows are importantly related to his own personal emotional well-being.[12]

PRINCIPLE 8: MODELING

Interviewed following the 1967 Six-Day War, Israeli Defense Minister Moshe Dayan was asked about the high officer casualty rate in the Israeli forces. He explained that in their army the officers led the way, in the first rank, ahead of the infantry companies. The interviewer, an experienced general, pointed out the danger that the army units would be left leaderless. Dayan replied that this was a calculated risk, but it was offset by the tremendous boost in morale to those in the ranks who saw their leader out in front, leading the way, setting the example.

What has now come to be called *modeling the role*, or *role model*, is found in many of the self-help groups. Put into simple terms, it means the leader gives a practical demonstration of the way he or she wants members to act within the group.

A.A. members go to visit the desperate alcoholic who has issued a cry for help. They don't lecture, they just tell the story of their own battle with alcohol and how they found a way out of it all. An alcoholic who is convinced attends a meeting and is bombarded with a barrage of personal experiences. "I am an alcoholic." "I have been dry for three years." "The fault never was with me." "I always blamed somebody else." "I discovered the program works." "I did the stupidest things." The frustrated alcoholic begins to feel better, and inwardly says, "These are my people." They too have been defeated and they found a way out of it—by following the plans. Maybe there is hope for change by trying it.

An exconvict stands before the prisoner soon to be released. He says, "I came here tonight in my air-conditioned Buick. When I leave I'm going to the Golden Ox to eat a steak. Then home to my wife, where we live in our nicely furnished apartment." He pauses, "I used to sleep in a cell and drink from my tin cup and dream about getting out. Then I faced reality. I realized I must work like fury against tremendous odds, if I were going to make it." Looking at this well-dressed businessman and hearing his story, the convict sees a possibility for life on the outside. This man's experience may trigger a motivation.

The drug addiction groups continually demonstrate role modeling. Newcomers to Daytop Lodge are informed right at the beginning that all the people in the house are former addicts. In the interview they are confronted with people who have been through it and are now managing without dope and doing well.

In Synanon the expression used is *role model*. The explanation is,

"The role model is a Synanist who has been in the situation of the newer person and has progressed to a higher level of performance. The role model is a living example of what the newcomer can become."

Of all the activities of the peer mutual self-help groups there is none more important then modeling the role. By this technique the group motivates others to follow the pathway of a life-enriching process.

PRINCIPLE 9: FAILURE IN SUCCESS

George Bernard Shaw is alleged to have said that the trouble with Jesus was that he had disciples. The difficulty with self-help groups is that they succeed, and that success often brings failure.

One by one, new movements have gone the same way. Methodism's class meeting disappeared as the church grew in strength; the Oxford Groups fought their way to acceptance, but in their development they changed from small groups.

Sometimes the problem is that groups are too rigid and don't change enough. Recovery, Inc., gives the impression that it jelled during Dr. Lowe's lifetime and has never changed or entertained a new idea since. It lacks flexibility and could do with an injection of new life and ideas.

A.A. has been painfully aware of these problems and has periodically reconsidered its organization. It lives in a constant horror that a bureaucractic structure may give it the "kiss of death." It stays with the one main purpose of working with alcoholics, refuses to accept outside support, and, while employing certain service personnel, will not be governed by them.

Peer mutual self-help groups are like people—they never stand still. They are constantly growing, developing, and deteriorating. They struggle for survival, they grow rapidly, but often once they are successful, they slow down, look with suspicion upon the new and untried, and become themselves followers of the dull, monotonous round to which they once so strenuously objected.

All too frequently when peer mutual self-help groups succeed, they really fail. Their only hope is constantly to learn anew, to drink from the fountain of eternal youth, and with an adventurous spirit be ready to try new and exciting ways of functioning.

IDEAS FOR GROUP FACILITATORS

Most people agree the principles of the self-help groups are fine and they commend them. How about measuring your own particular group against these self-help principles?

Make some copies of this chart, and have each member of your group take a copy and evaluate the group's performance.

SELF-HELP PRINCIPLES RATING CHART

	Always	Generally	Sometimes	Occasionally	Never
SOCIALIZATION Our group makes participants feel they are accepted in a warn, loving climate.					
RESPONSIBILITY We insist members quit blaming others and accept responsibility for their behavior.					
HIGH STANDARDS We help people live up to their own value systems.					

SLOGANS AND EPIGRAMS
Members often use easily remembered statements of principles when talking in groups.

LAY LEADERSHIP
We encourage lay people to move into positions of leadership.

CONFESSION
Within our group it is easy for people to become open and confess their failures.

BEHAVIOR
We insist people speak of acts rather than feelings.

RESTITUTION
When someone has hurt someone else, we insist on some type of restitution.

	Always	Generally	Sometimes	Occasionally	Never

HELPING OTHERS

Believing "You cannot
keep your experience
unless you give it away,"
we encourage members
to move toward
helping each other.

MODELING

Group members help
others by telling of their
own failures and their
recovery of relationship.

PROCESSES

In one sense considering the principles of the peer mutual self-helpers before examining their practices is putting the cart before the horse. The groups have been actionists and have spent very little time theorizing and formulating principles. Turning now to processes, we get to the heart of the matter—the way in which the self-help groups function. The following chapters will use many hypothetical situations to illustrate these processes.

7. Initiation into the Group

MICHAEL DUNCAN is sitting rather apprehensively in the somewhat shabby reception room of an equally shabby two-story building to which he has come in the hope of getting some help with his drug problem. A young man appears at the door and invites Michael into an adjoining office, where another young man is seated. As they introduce themselves as Hank and Jay, Michael mentally notes they are probably social workers.

Hank and Jay don't waste any time; they ask Michael point blank why he shoots dope. In response Michael tells his often repeated story of the unfortunate environment of childhood days, the sorry family in which he had been nurtured, and all the bad breaks he has had in life.

"Hey, stop this garbage. Who do you think you're talking to?"

The two interviewers speak to each other: "Did you ever hear such s - - - in your life!"

"This dope fiend thinks he's inside another joint."

"He didn't get enough affection and love from his mudder and fodder, I bet."[1]

In the course of the discussion that follows, the interviewers make it clear that they themselves are reformed addicts. They have behaved in exactly the same way Michael has, so there is nothing to be gained by using his usual techniques to try to manipulate them. They keep needling and pushing him until he is at last willing to acknowledge his own responsibility, to admit that his stupidity brought on his trouble. Once having made this admission, and indicating he is anxious to undertake a radical restructuring his life, Michael is ready to start on a new type of life in this program.

This example is an extreme form of intake procedure utilized by a self-help group. But it illustrates the fundamental emphasis of self-helpers on the use of peers, former addicts in this instance, to do the interviewing; modeling, by group members' telling of their own experiences; and accepting personal responsibility as a condition for entering a self-help group.

The peer mutual self-help psychotherapy groups use a great variety of styles in what is called the intake interview. In this chapter, we will focus on the methods used with individuals in one counseling center utilizing Integrity Therapy. In the next chapter we will consider an intake for marriage counseling.

DO YOU HAVE YOUR EARS ON?

The Citizens' Band radio operators have developed a whole new vocabulary for the processes of communication. One of their most picturesque expressions is that used to find out if a driver's receiver is turned on and functioning: "Do you have your ears on?" Any counselor must have his or her ears on at all times, for, as the Desiderata says, ". . . listen to others, even the dull and the ignorant; they have their story."

Experience has shown that intake interviewers following self-help principles all too easily fail to listen. Excited about their own experience, sometimes they can hardly bear to let someone else talk; they have never learned to really listen. These eager beavers all too frequently overtalk the troubled person and fail to develop rapport; the newcomer doesn't get the feeling of satisfaction that comes when someone is willing to listen. In all types of counseling, listening is of the utmost importance. A good rule of thumb is for the interviewer to spend two thirds of the available time listening.

INTRODUCING THE RESPONSIBILITY CONCEPT

After listening to the counselees' stories the counselor begins the delicate task of leading them to accept some responsibility for their present condition. This is not easy. Most of us wish to maintain that if something has gone wrong, it is because of what someone else has done. Like the child who turns on a parent with, "Why did you make me do that?", most of us practice what is sometimes called the art of blamesmanship. The interviewer counters this attitude by pointing out that few of us get into trouble because of what others did to us. No matter how unfortunate our circumstances are, we individually made some wrong move.

Many counselees will want to dwell on symptoms: "I have a sick headache," "This low back pain bothers me," "I feel anxious all the time." The counselor's response is to show the counselee that these uncomfortable symptoms may be surface manifestations of underlying irresponsibilities and it is necessary to discover the root from which they come. In Integrity Therapy terms, some personal violation of values is probably the cause.

Although this statement may make the procedure sound rather simple, in actual practice it is quite difficult. It calls for a special skill. Psychiatrist William Glasser, describing his work with delinquent girls, tells of a prostitute who had built up a careful rationalization of her behavior. Finally Glasser asked the girl if she would want her daughter to be a prostitute and she said No, thus passing judgment on her own activity.

As a part of the discussion, the counselor may introduce the basic concepts of Integrity Therapy. In our counseling center we often refer to the *Little Red Book*,[2] a small pamphlet summarizing the principles of Integrity Therapy. The interviewing counselor makes particular mention of three principles:

1. All individuals have a conscience, or value system, and when they violate this conscience they become guilty. Guilt is not a sickness but a result of their wrongdoing and irresponsibility.

2. A common reaction to personal wrongdoing is to cover up and deny the experience. In this secrecy guilt gives rise to symptoms that may upset the balance of life.

3. As secrecy causes people's troubles and separates them from others, so openness is the beginning point on the road back to normality. This openness begins with one person, then moves to "significant others."

The counselor concludes the presentation of these ideas and then moves naturally into the technique of modeling the role to demonstrate to the counselees a practical application of the theory.

MODELING THE ROLE

This first part of the interview has proceeded on the cognitive level but now the counselor moves naturally into the experiential level.

Many group leaders do not function effectively because of what Yalom calls a need to be perfect. In Integrity Thebapy competent leaders must be willing to admit their own frailty in the technique referred to as modeling the role. Support for this concept has come from the field of behavior modification, where practitioners point out that some skills cannot be learned by trial and error or even reinforcing techniques. Albert Bandura makes the point:

It is highly doubtful, for example, that an experimenter could teach a mynah bird the phrase "successive approximations" by selective reinforcement of the bird's random squeaks and squawks. On the other hand, housewives establish extensive verbal repertoires in their feathered friends by verbally modeling desired phrases either in person or by means of recordings. Similarly, if children had no exposure to verbalizing models it would probably be impossible to teach them the kinds of verbal responses that constitute a language. In cases involving intricate patterns of behavior, modeling is an indispensable aspect of learning.[3]

Yalom points out the special possibilities for the group leader using the modeling techniques: "Despite these provocative possibilities, it is the therapist who willingly or unwillingly will continue to serve as the chief model-setting figure for the group patients."[4]

Dr. O. Hobart Mowrer popularized the technique. Mowrer tells how, after traumatic experiences in his own life in which he discovered the great help of becoming open, he would tell his story to an acquaintance, who would respond, "There are some things about me that you probably don't know." These experiences led Mowrer to ask:

If I can talk honestly about myself and cause these essentially normal individuals to "open up" would it not be possible to use the same approach, as a deliberate therapeutic gesture, with persons who are in real trouble and desperately need to expand their sphere of openness and "ethical sincerity"?[5]

Thus was born the concept of modeling the role.

Let us look in on a case where the counselor is following the technique of modeling the role, and notice the method of a pastor who uses Integrity Therapy in his counseling. The pastor has been chosen as an example because pastors, of all people, generally have the greatest difficulty in admitting failure and shortcoming and are often shocked by the suggestion that they be willing to share such experiences with a parishioner.

Mrs. Lynda Scott called her minister and requested an appointment, so Rev. Sam Harris made arrangements to see her at 2 P.M. the following afternoon. Preliminaries over and done with, Mrs. Scott begins to pour out her tale of woe. "I went to see my doctor last week. I have been having these horrible headaches and an uneasy feeling that something terrible is going to happen to me.

"For some time now the children have been worrying me and my husband is certainly not understanding. I decided there must be something wrong with me physically, you know I've heard all those television commercials about tired blood and iron deficiency so I decided to have a checkup.

"After all these tests the doctor told me he couldn't find a thing wrong with me. He suggested I might need to see a psychiatrist. That certainly shocked me. I contemplated going to another doctor to make sure the first one had not made a mistake. Then I heard that you did some counseling so I decided to come and see you."

Sam Harris smiles. "I'm so glad you felt free to come and call on me. And I think you were very wise to go and have a medical checkup to make sure there was no physical basis for your difficulties.

"We operate on a slightly different basis here from other counseling centers. We feel the most important single reason we get into difficulty is because we fail to live by our values. When we do not live by our values our conscience gets after us and brings on what we call symptoms. If there is no physical basis for your malaise, it might well be that your conscience is trying to call attention to the places where you have failed.

"You know, we have all failed somewhere, and when I see you I understand something of what you are passing through because of an experience I had myself. In this church we have a highly organized visitation program. I have promoted this program very vigorously and urged my church members to participate. But I do not find it easy to call on people myself, so every Thursday evening I always find some excuse not to go. A sermon to prepare, or a sick call to make, or a committe meeting to attend; and sometimes I would just feel sick myself.

"One Thursday night I was sitting at home watching television and the door bell rang. When I answered it there stood two of my church members who were out visiting and had called at our house by mistake. They caught me. I was in my old slacks, T-shirt, and sneakers. I made some sort of lame excuse about not feeling well, and after they'd gone I developed a horrible headache. From that time on whenever I'd get up at church supper and promote the church visitation program my head would start to ache.

"You see, Mrs. Scott, I had been acting irresponsibly and my conscience was speaking to me through my headaches. Is there any possibility that your difficulties may stem back to some failure on your part?"

Mrs. Scott has been sitting in silence and doesn't answer for some time. Then she says, "Well there is something that I know that I should not. . . ." And out comes a story of personal failure.

In this process the counselor takes a calculated risk. His counselee may not respond. However, he has taken the initiative to open the way for an interchange between himself and the counselee. He proceeds, "I would like to invite you to join a group of people who meet each week. We are all failures and we are working to help each other."

Many counselees are apprehensive about joining groups and may need to ask the interviewers some questions. It might be desirable for the interviewer to volunteer some information about the nature of the group experience. One very effective interviewer says:

You'll probably find your participation in our group something not quite like any experience you ever had before. You'll find these people are really sharing with you and with one another, sharing secrets about themselves that may be shocking to you, and sometimes deeply upsetting. There will be many moments in the group experience when you will feel anxious, put upon and perhaps compelled to defend yourself. Maybe you'll even be tempted to withdraw or leave. But I hope you won't. I hope you'll stay and that you'll listen and realize that these people are doing what they are doing because they care about one another and about you—because they are concerned. Concerned in wiser and better ways, perhaps, than people have ever been concerned about you before. I hope that you'll stay, too, because I know that when you are able to work through the anxiety you will discover in the group a new joy, and new strength, and a new kind of living that you've never known before. I can almost promise you it will be worth every bit of the anxiety and difficulty you may go through to get it.[6]

If the counselee agrees to join the group, it is the practice in one counseling center to introduce a contract like that shown below, which is simply a commitment to participate for at least six weeks. However it is done, the counselee should make a commitment and arrange a time and place for meetings.

COUNSELING AGREEMENT

Understanding that Integrity Therapy has an implication of honesty and commitment, I undertake to become a part of a therapy group meeting each Tuesday at 7:00 P.M. I further make this commitment to attend for at least six weeks commencing _____ and continuing until _____.

Name _____

Address _____

City & Zip _____

Witness _____

INTRODUCTION TO THE GROUP

Let us review what is happening in this intake process. In the example of Mrs. Scott, the individual is troubled because she has been isolating herself from others and "putting up a front." In this interview she has commenced being open and shared her experiences of failure with one person, the interviewer. However, it is necessary that the process go beyond just two people.

One way of further extending the experience of openness is for several people to do the interviewing. Dr. Mowrer tells about his Integrity groups in which a committee of four conducts an intake interview, which may last for two or more hours. It is easy to see the rationale for this; however, in a large counseling center with as many as fifteen intake interviews in one evening, it is not too practical.

The answer we have found is to ask certain group members to be ready to work as intakers. Members so designated sit down with prospective group members and go through the intake procedure. The intaker goes to the group with those who decide to join, and at the appropriate time, introduces the new members and helps them get started. An example of the way this is done is seen in the hypothetical case of James Hatton who readily responded to his intake interviewer, Wayne Cunningham.

HATTON: I've got some apprehensions about going into a group, but you sound pretty convincing and I guess I ought to try it.

CUNNINGHAM: I think I can understand your concern, but I am delighted you've decided to come to groups and I am going to accompany you and be with you for at least the first session.

HATTON: Thanks. I'm sure that will be a help.

Cunningham and Hatton proceed to the group already in progress under the direction of the group leader.

LEADER: We are delighted to have you with us. Harry is just telling us about a difficulty in relating to his mother-in-law.

After Harry is through, the leader turns to Hatton and asks him to tell the group something about himself.

HATTON: My name is James Hatton, and I think I'd rather just sit here and observe how it all goes.

James' introduction to the group has reached a critical point. One principle of the group is "No spectators, only participators." If this principle is simply stated, it may create a difficult situation, but Wayne Cunningham is ready.

CUNNINGHAM: I did the interview with James. James, why don't you let me help you? I suggest you share with us about these difficulties with your teenage daughter.

Wayne proceeds to lead James along and give him the feeling that he has a friend in the group who is there to help him. Periodically Wayne asks James questions geared toward evoking a response.

The intake interview with an individual is the beginning of the process of resocialization. In this experience counselors may have to allay some of the new members' fears. Sometimes counselees will seek to con the interviewer by saying such things as, "I am sure you are very competent; I would be happy to have one-to-one counseling with you, but I don't much care for the idea of groups." This is a stern test, as counselors learn whether they can withstand flattery and live by their convictions. They may need to tell the counselees it is their conviction that a group will do a much more effective job than one-to-one counseling. On other occasions they may need to describe just what will happen within a group. In any case when counselors accompany new group members to the group, they may perform some of the most effective functions in getting newcomers underway in a new experience of relationship.

Initiatory rites are an important part of entering a club, organization, or society and are intended to introduce the initiate into a new set of obligations and privileges. One definition of initiate is "to admit with formal rites into secret knowledge, a society, etc." There are no formal rites in peer mutual self-help groups, but the intake interview is an initiatory experience in which the new knowledge is, "We alone can do it, but we cannot do it alone." Subjects will certainly enter a new society in which they will learn a whole new way of life as members of a therapeutic group. With so much at stake, intake interviewers must do their work with care and concern.

IDEAS FOR GROUP FACILITATORS

One of the biggest problems in group activities is getting the members acquainted with each other. No group can reach any depth unless the members feel comfortable together. The more rapidly the members come to feel at ease and share confidence with each other, the sooner the group will get down to work.

The technique suggested here involves a few simple materials for each participant:

1. An 8½" × 11" sheet of paper.
2. A pencil.
3. A safety pin or some other means of attaching the paper to the clothing.

Explain the reason for the experience to the group: "I am anxious that we all get to know each other as soon as possible. To do this we are going to play a little game we might call 'Who Am I?' this will take us through a series of steps:

1. "You will each write on the top of your sheet 'Who Am I?' and then list ten answers. Make sure you write clearly and legibly.
2. "After you have completed your sheet, fasten it on to the front of your clothing.
3. "You are to mix around, making sure you stand in front of each other member of the group for at least two minutes

without talking. As you meet each other member, you will stand looking first of all in the individual's eyes and then at his or her ten statements.

4. "Every two minutes I will give you a signal to move on.

5. "At the conclusion of this experience you may go and talk with three people whom you found to be particularly interesting.

6. "At the conclusion of this period each member will hang his or her sheet of paper on the wall.

7. "We will reassemble in a circle and will share, in turn, what we discovered through this experience."

8. Marriage Counseling—Similar but Different

MARRIAGE IS primarily an experience of union and affiliation in which two people commit themselves to share life together. In their relationship they reveal more of their inner life to each other than they have ever before shown to another person. As children arrive and the family expands, ideally there are increasing possibilities for close relationship with an ever expanding number of people.

Unfortunately, marriage doesn't always reach this ideal level. Most problems of married life arise in the realm of relationship and communication. After the initial romance diminishes and with the realization that expectation may never be fulfilled, communication may deteriorate until it reaches a stage in which two embattled partners may take refuge behind psychological defenses, only occasionally sallying forth on an offensive sortie against the spouse. Legally living together in the same house, walking the same carpets, and even sleeping in the same bed, they are emotionally divorced.

The profession of marriage counseling has arisen in an effort to heal the hurt of ruptured matrimonial relationships. In the main its work has been conducted on a one-to-one basis; dissatisfaction with results has led to some experimentation with variations on the technique.

In conjoint therapy the partners have joint sessions with the therapist, who is able to see the interaction between them and evaluate the quality of the relationship. The therapist works along with them in a program in which they learn new ways to relate to each other. A disadvantage of this method is that either or both partners may become cagey about what is said in the presence of the other. When either is frank and open, the other spouse sometimes becomes oversensitive and later accuses, "You said thus and so when we were with the counselor." The charge had been more devastating because it was made in the presence of a third person.

Another variation, called collaborative therapy, provides a therapist for each spouse. The therapists periodically confer and discuss the developments, obtaining what they call the stereoscopic effect for evaluating progress from the perspective of both participants.

While these efforts certainly have been a step in the right direction, it seems obvious that if marriage difficulties are mainly problems of affinity, the logical and the best strategy will be to deal with them in the context of relationships where the partners can learn new interpersonal skills. Working with ruptured marriage, Integrity Therapy takes the position that "by relationships they were hurt and by relationships they shall be healed." Let us look at an intake interview with a husband and wife based on this principle.

ASSESSING THE SITUATION

When two people arrive at a counseling center to discuss a problem in their marriage, it isn't easy to tell what motivations brought them. Quite frequently one has come reluctantly, so the first task is to discover who is most willing to talk. As they sit with the counselor, it generally becomes clear who is cooperative and who reluctant. If a wife says, "Go on, you tell him, you're the one who wanted to come," the counselor realizes that she is not going to be the best person to supply information about the situation. The counselor suggests that the least communicative partner wait in the reception room, and tries to learn the background of the situation from the more talkative spouse. When enough information has been gained the talkative spouse waits in the reception room while the counselor interviews the other partner.

A variation of this method is to have two intake interviewers, each talking with one of the partners individually. At the conclusion of each interview, the two interviewers consult together about the next step in the process.

ACCEPTING RESPONSIBILITY

At an individual counseling interview, the counselor spends at least two thirds of the available time listening, and generally speaks only to ask a question aimed at gaining new information or clarifying what is being said. This is generally a time in which the interviewee recounts the difficulties of the marriage relationship as he or she sees it. This session is characteristically marked by complaints about the absent spouse's behavior.

The skill of the interviewer is demonstrated by the way in which she or he guides the counselee into accepting some responsibility for the situation. The philosophy underlying this stage is that in any relationship between two people in which there are problems, no one individual is altogether wrong, nor is the other altogether right. The problem is to persuade a counselee that this is so. In our counseling center we have worked on the basis that most people are willing to accept at least 10 percent of the blame.

In our hypothetical interview, Rev. Tom Jackson sits talking with a church member who had called earlier and made an appointment. Obviously under considerable emotional pressure, Mrs. Towery is telling about some of the difficulties and frustrations of married life: "I find it hard to talk about my marriage, but I've had such horrible depressions, and I know I must do something about it all. It has taken me weeks to make up my mind and now I feel as if I am being disloyal to Eric.

"Although we have been coming to this church for years, you have never really known Eric. He attends church pretty regularly, but I am afraid he's not really a very good husband.

"He is thoughtless, does very little to help around the house, and because his work takes him away so much, he does not accept his responsibility with the children."

The pastor-counselor has been listening attentively and tries to reflect back some of the emotions his troubled parishioner is expressing.

"You feel Eric has not fulfilled his obligations as a husband should?"

"That's exactly how I feel and it's getting me down. These periods of depression are getting worse, and the reason I came to see you is to ask your help. Do you think there is some way you could talk to Eric and urge him to be a better husband and father?"

"I'm sorry, Mrs. Towery, I don't know how I could do that. But there is another way of coming at it."

"Oh?"

"Yes. There are two people in a marriage; it is a shared enterprise, and when something snarls it up it is never just a matter of one person being wrong and the other person being right."

"Well . . . er, I guess that is so."

"Let us work from this basis and take your marriage, for example. I can see how badly your husband has acted. But let us suppose your husband is 90 percent wrong. Would you be willing to accept 10 percent of the blame for the difficulties that you presently face?"

Mrs. Towery considers this for some time then responds, "Well, maybe 10 percent; but he is the major factor in our present difficulty."

"All right. But we don't have your husband here at the moment—how about if we start on your 10 percent?"

If all the time is spent discussing Mr. Towery, it may give the wife a sense of satisfaction; but Mr. Towery is not present, so nothing can change him. The counselor has persuaded Mrs. Towery to accept some responsibility for the situation, and so she has taken a step of major importance.

REVIEWING THE PRINCIPLES

Tom Jackson takes up the conversation again. "We practice a form of counseling called Integrity Therapy, and to oversimplify it, we believe that when we fail to live by our value system our conscience troubles us and gives rise to symptoms—symptoms like backaches, headaches, and even depression.

"If we accept this theory we can say that this has happened to you. Now tell me, where would you say your greatest failure has been?"

Mrs. Towery looks a little startled, sinks into silence, then slowly answers, "I guess I've failed in a number of places but I've been so busy blaming Eric that I find it difficult to face my own failures. This isn't quite what I expected when I came here, and it's not going to be easy for me to get used to thinking this way."

"Let me help you then. Are you a good housekeeper? If I called on you unexpectedly would you be pleased to welcome me into your house?"

Mrs. Towery shrugs her shoulders. "I don't suppose I'm too bad, but then I'm not as good as I should be."

Mrs. Towery has now become specific about one area of irresponsibility. Housework is a very mundane task, but once she admits to some area of failure she may be ready to move into some of the more important areas of life.

MODELING

Having made an effort to lead the counselee into accepting at least a minimum of responsibility, the interviewer relates an incident of personal irresponsibility and tells of the way in which it affected him. This means he is willing to share the story of his own failure with his counseler, who can now feel at ease in relating her own experiences.

The pastor-counselor continues with the discussion.

"I suppose most church members have a pretty good opinion of their minister, but we have our faults too. Being human, I often make mistakes, but I discover that when I do I get into trouble. When I was invited to be a committee member on the United Fund I was delighted because I believed the church should be involved in social service. As time went on, I found myself spending more and more time on these committee activities to the detriment of my church responsibilities. The trouble was that I had met a lot of leading lights of the city, and I became part of a whirl of social activities. Then one day my deacons had a special meeting and told me how concerned they were that I had little time for church work, and my sermons were indicating my lack of preparation. I was infuriated. I blamed the church, said they didn't appreciate my ministry. But when I cooled off, in my saner moments I realized it wasn't the church, it was I who was wrong. It is always easy to blame someone else. Does your experience have any sort of parallel with mine?"

Mrs. Towery sits in silence for a few minutes, then begins to speak. "Well I suppose if I really want to help I should be honest. . . ."

The distinction between modeling in individual counseling and modeling in marriage counseling is the emphasis on *relationship*. Individuals must accept responsibility for their own failures; in marriage counseling one spouse must be taught to quit blaming the conveniently available partner and accept responsibility for a portion of the problem. No matter how badly one partner has behaved, there is always some fault on the part of the so called innocent spouse, and the task of the counselor is to evoke a response of this order.

The whole procedure is repeated with the other partner. Once again there is an insistence that there be an acknowledgement of at least some responsibility for the deteriorated relationship.

THE CONTRACT

If the husband and wife both give some indication of a willingness to work on the problem, the counselor invites them to join therapy groups. At this point the contract is introduced. They are already involved in the contract they entered with their marriage vows; now they're entering into a contract to really do something about the problems that are presently confronting the marriage.

After the spouses have each signed the contract, a decision is made as to which particular group they will join. Careful consideration is given to this placement in an effort to put them with peers with regard to sex, age, and type of problem. As much as possible, the intake interviewer accompanies the new member to the group. This procedure is most practical when two counselors were involved, each doing the intake for one spouse.

An intake interview is of the utmost importance and should be undertaken with great care. It sets the stage for all that is to follow. Upon this interview may rest the responsibility for preparing the way for a meaningful counseling experience.

IDEAS FOR GROUP FACILITATORS

Many husbands and wives are unhappy in their relationships but are not quite sure why. The following exercise is aimed at helping both of them pinpoint some of the reasons for dissatisfaction.

Instructions: Spouses are to list in two columns, "What I want from this marriage," and "What I am willing to contribute to this marriage." They should state the items in behavioral terms:

NOT " I want him to respect me."
BUT " I want him to ask my opinion before making a decision."

NOT " I want her to be more conscientious."
BUT " I would like her to fix breakfast for me in the morning."

After each spouse has completed the chart, the counselor can sit down with them and discuss the sensitive areas.

What I Want from This Marriage	What I Am Willing to Contribute to This Marriage

≋ 9. Establishing a Group

AN EVENT of the greatest magnitude may have just taken place with such little notice that the time has come to call attention to it. A news item has informed us of a unique wedding ceremony. The bride, in a blue pick-up truck, drove down the aisle formed by guests' cars. Some distance away, across the supermarket parking lot, the preacher, who is known to the Citizens' Band fraternity by his handle "Sky Pilot," spoke into his microphone. "Earl Yowell, alias 'Little Ripoff,' do you take Anita Cole—'Little Stinger'—to be your lawfully wedded wife?" So to the strange modern settings for weddings—while roller skating, jumping from an airplane, dancing, has been added another, based on a current craze—Citizens' Band radio.

Only a few years ago I speculated about the way the automobile had apparently become the last outpost of individuality. In other forms of transportation—bus, train, or plane—traveling is a shared enterprise; but not so with the automobile. As one man asked at a social function, "Come on now, admit it. What tightwad family all came in one car?"

When the Russian leader Nikita Khrushchev visited the United States and watched the cars streaming down a San Francisco freeway, his critical comment was that so many cars with just one driver were an awful waste of transportation. It seemed to me that the car might have become the logical descendent of the cowboy's bronco. Like that noble beast it usually carries one person; any additional passengers are only taken under special circumstances. The automobile driver is cut off from other people and out of communication with them.

Now I'm going to have to eat my words. This last bastion of individual privacy has fallen before the onslaught of the CB radio. Just switch on a CB receiver and listen to all the chit-chat and the esoteric language that fills the airwaves as CBers exchange greetings and warnings of local yokel (city police) county mounties (sheriffs or deputies) or smokey bears (state troopers). Some CBers tell complete strangers where they come from, where they are going, and many details of their lives they wouldn't normally dream of discussing with people they had never met. CB communication leaps across class barriers and the humblest citizen may finish up talking with former first lady Betty Ford, who has the handle Big Mama.

Self-help groups have many resemblances to the CB world. A sense of belonging to a special group of people, the anonymity in which life's situations are discussed, learning new ways of communicating, the joyous discovery that there are people who are willing, in CB language, to put their ears on. The biggest problem in both CB and self-help groups appears to be getting started. Would-be CBers generally need to be with some friendly, experienced person who can help to initiate them to this new world of the airwaves, just as people conscious of needing a deep personal relationship with others are apprehensive about how to get started in group life.

WHERE ARE THE GROUPS?

As we have already indicated, the initial intake interview will be the introduction to a new era of relationship and commitment to attending a group. But which group?

Rev. James Sullivan has been talking with Mrs. McKinney and has recommended that she join a group. Mrs. McKinney considers the matter carefully and at last reaches a decision. "I think I would like to join a group such as you describe, but where would I find one?"

The pastor now finds himself in a dilemma. Where can he find such a group?

The most obvious way to experienced pastor–promoters is to make a series of announcements to their congregation about the formation of a group. Or they might possibly convert some already existing organization in the church to this purpose. In both cases there will be difficulties because they will frequently find themselves with uninterested or curious but poorly motivated people.

Probably the simplest thing would be for Rev. Sullivan to involve his wife. Many a pastor's wife would jump at the opportunity to assist her husband with his counseling. The pastor could invite his wife to join with him and Mrs. McKinney, and they would immediately be in business as a group. Three people constitute a group—a small one, with not a great many possibilities of interaction—but nevertheless a group.

It will not be long before other people begin making inquiries, and the group starts to grow. So it might be well to decide early on the size of the group. The minimum, of course, will be three; once it grows to as many as ten, the group should probably split. With two groups of five, the pastor could take one and his wife, the other.

The next question is whether a group should be open or closed. *Closed* groups are those in which the members all begin at the same time, sometimes committing themselves to come for a given period. The advantages of this type of group include the knowledge that the members originating it are going to be together for a certain time, the provision of a stable environment in which members can develop loyalty and reciprocity, and the freedom from the threat that may come with the arrival of strangers.

But *open* groups, such as we are advocating, have their own advantages. The number of group members will fluctuate, the older members in the group are more experienced and provide models for the newcomers. As newcomers arrive, they sometimes bring a new challenge and help to prevent a feeling of staleness that sometimes descends upon groups. From my own wide experience I will opt for open groups.

When groups are small, the composition is not very important; but as the number of members grows it becomes a greater consideration. The case for groups of both sexes, husbands and wives together, can be very compelling. If the group is a microcosm, or small world, then it will be a situation in which men and women will be working together. However, in a series of studies carried out in our center comparing couples' groups to those that were exclusively male or female, we found members of the couples' group didn't do nearly as well as those in groups separated by sex. People often enjoyed being in couples' groups, and in retrospect said they were enjoyable or nice, in much the same way as they might have referred to a visit to the movies or some social event. The main problem was that in group interaction, couples often acted in a cagey manner, looking at a spouse when talking as if to say, "is this all right?" They all too frequently failed to get down to business and rarely become open and frank about the real difficulties of their relationship.

Our conclusion is that most people do best in peer groups; men speak best to men, women to women, boys to boys, and girls to girls. The family experiencing difficulty that comes to the counseling center as a family unit is counseled in the context of a peer group (see Figure 14). Each of the family members is interviewed individually then assigned to a group of peers—the father with men, mother with women, teenage boy with adolescent boys, teenage girl with adolescent girls. The leaders of the respective groups confer as to the progress of each of the family members so they can share each other's perspective. The family members, for their part, return to the home, which becomes a laboratory in which they practice the skills they learned in their groups. The following week they return to their peer groups to report their experiences, and each leader, with the knowledge of the commitments made by the other family members, is able to evaluate progress.

The setting in which the group meets is of little importance. Some groups like to sit around a table, others see a table as a barrier to free interchange and discussion. The main consideration is privacy. No interruptions; no telephones or children. Some groups drink coffee, but we don't like this. Similarly we have no smoking. Any of these practices can be distracting and frequently offer a way of escape for people who try to avoid a group situation they find threatening.

When will your groups meet? Think carefully about this before making a definite decision. Most busy pastors already have enough nights out and many women can more conveniently come in the daytime. However, if you hope to have men, then you should meet in the evening. No one time will ever suit everybody, so decide on the best time for most people, and those who really want to come will find a way to be there.

STRUCTURING THE SESSION

Group structuring can take different forms. Following are both the "ground rules" and the "ten commandments" of Mowrer's Integrity groups, which differ slightly from Integrity Therapy groups.

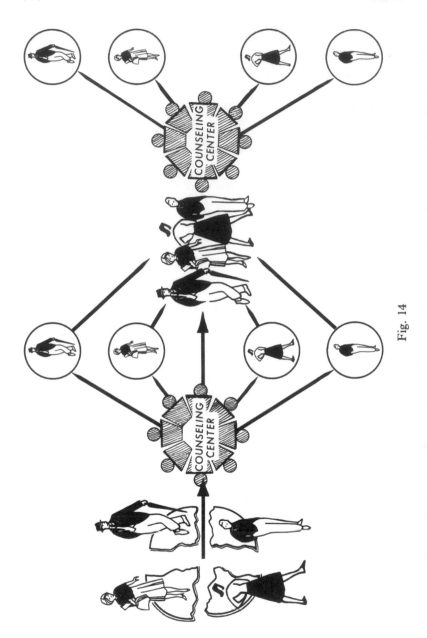

Fig. 14

GROUND RULES OF MOWRER'S INTEGRITY GROUPS[1]

1. There are no threats or carrying out of physical violence.
2. No one leaves a group session to avoid being upset or challenged.
3. There is no ganging up on a member or giving unwarranted emotional support.
4. There are no restrictions on the verbal or nonverbal language group members may employ.
5. There is no subgrouping in or outside of the group to drain off issues that should be shared with the total group.
6. Confidentiality is binding on all, except that group members are free to talk about their own group participation to people outside the group.
7. All new members are expected to subscribe to the core values of honesty, responsibility, and involvement and to practice these in and outside of the group.

THE "TEN COMMANDMENTS" OF MOWRER'S INTEGRITY GROUPS[2]

1. *Don't interrupt!* Show the other person the courtesy of listening to him. He will certainly feel better if you "hear him out" instead of interrupting him.

2. *Don't blame!* You rarely change other people by complaining about them, no matter how much "at fault" they may be. But if *you* change, so also will their reaction to you.

3. *Don't "act-off" negative emotions* (e.g., resentment, jealousy, depression, etc.)! "Coming out sideways," in the form of sarcasm, wise cracks, put-downs, or indirect attacks is a common form of "acting-off." Sometimes sideways behavior passes as clever or witty but can wound, oneself as well as others.

4. *Don't "one-on-one"!* If you are up-tight or baffled about something (i.e., need help), by all means telephone or talk individually with one or more members of your group (and later report this in your group). But don't argue or fight verbally. Another form of "one-on-oneing" occurs in a group when two persons talk or whisper to each other rather than listening to and participating in what is going on in the group as a whole. This is sometimes called *sub-grouping.*

5. *Don't "Yes . . . but"!* If you are trying to effect a recon-
ciliation with (get rid of resentments toward) someone, the first
question to ask is: "What contribution did *I* make to this situation?"
When you've seen *your* error, "cop to it." But you'll lose the whole
game if you say: "Yes, I did thus and so, *but* . . ." and then proceed to justify, alibi, disavow your accountability, your responsibility. Instead, simply say, "I did it. I goofed. I'm sorry, wish to
make amends, and will not do it again." Period.

6. *Don't "talk back"!* At Daytop Village and in Integrity Groups,
the correct response to a "pull-up" (being caught and corrected
when you are off base) is "Thank you!" You'll never start an argument or fight with this response. If, upon reflection, you think the
pull-up was unwarranted, run it *in group* with the other person.

7. *Don't mind-read—or expect others to do so!* Let the other
person state his own position and take the responsibility for having
done so, as you yourself are expected to do. Don't try to second-
guess him (especially as a means of justifying what you *want* to
believe or do), or expect him to second-guess you.

8. *Don't fudge!* If you have an agreement with another person,
keep it—or else renegotiate the agreement, *before* rather than after
you violate it.

9. *Don't double-talk!* Language is a precious gift, don't abuse
it: by deliberately deceiving, playing wordy games, being incon-
sistent, self-contradictory, or evasive. Respect the connection
between words and reality.

10. *Don't tit-for-tat!* When another person challenges you on
some aspect of your behavior, it is better to accept the challenge
(if valid) and mend your ways than to try to nullify the challenge by
reminding the other person of some of *his* shortcomings.

Once people are seated, the leader should commence by stating
the limits under which the group functions. For instance:

"We want to welcome you here this evening. So that there will be
no misunderstanding I want you to know some of the principles under
which this group operates.

"1. We are gathered here under *the covenant of confidentiality*. This
means that no one repeats outside the group anything that is said as
we are gathered here. Every individual tells his own story—not someone else's.

"2. There are no spectators, only participators. Everyone here is under an obligation to participate. If you have just come to have a look, then you are in the wrong place.

"3. We have all failed. There are no perfect people in our groups. We don't discuss our strong points—we speak about our weaknesses. We have a saying: 'A man is never stronger than when he is admitting his weaknesses.'

"4. Before we can tell anybody what he should do in his situation, we must 'earn the right.' We earn the right by admitting our own failures before we tell anybody else his failures.

"5. Because we are operating under the covenant of confidentiality, it is not necessary that we know each other's last names, so we will function on a first-name basis.

"6. Our group will run for two hours. We commence at 7 P.M. sharp and we try to stop at exactly 9 P.M., so let us use the time wisely."

Having structured the group the leader now models the role—sets the example—saying, for instance:

"We are going to have a session of 'hopes and fears.' This period will be conducted without any comment from the group. Each member should make a short statement about his or her greatest hopes and greatest fears.

"My greatest hope is that I will be able to be open about my failures and discuss them with this group, and my greatest fear is that I will not succeed in communicating my concern and that I may not be able to make a contribution to the group.

"Let us now proceed around the circle. Jim . . ."

Following "hopes and fears," leaders can then begin with their own story and tell of an experience of irresponsibility, at the conclusion turning to one of the group and saying "Now Harry why don't you tell us about yourself?" or "Well, Harry, *who* are you?"

So the group is born. Like any birth it should be natural and relatively easy. It is, in fact, fraught with hazards, but generally not as many as might have been anticipated.

NOT-SO-WELCOMED VISITORS TO GROUP

Psychiatric Sam—Wants to diagnose every situation. He leads the group into the "paralysis of analysis."

Prosecuting Priscilla—Attacks people with a whole series of questions. She's been reading too many "who dunnits."

Self-Righteous Cyril—He cannot think of any mistakes that he has ever made. Apparently everyone else in the world has failed, but he really wants to spend the time polishing up his halo.

Talkative Thomas—Always has something to say about every subject under discussion. He knows a little bit about everything and therefore feels that he has to constantly keep on talking.

Retiring Rose—She modestly maintains that she doesn't want to waste the group's time and feels that they could move on to give someone else a chance to talk. This is just a cover-up because she does not really want to participate.

Helpful Harry—When he sees that another group member is feeling the heat, especially in an area where he is vulnerable, he helps his comrade with such a statement as, "We all do that don't we?" Implicitly he hopes the other will come to his rescue later when he is facing a difficult situation.

Poor Pete—Always feels sorry for himself.

Hopeless Hannah—She has an insoluble problem. It doesn't matter what is suggested, she has either tried it or it won't work.

Most group leaders find themselves periodically faced with the problem of making sure the available time is wisely used. One way to do this is to allocate a certain amount of time to each group member. The leader may say, "We have two hours—120 minutes—and we want to use the time wisely. As there are ten of us, we each have twelve minutes. We'll go around making sure each person has an opportunity for his or her twelve minutes. After everybody has spoken, we will use the time left over for someone who needs it." This statement is not an immutable law, but it means the leader can stop someone who is overstepping the mark with the warning, "You remember our agreement; you've had your twelve minutes. Let's move on." If, on the other hand, there's a case of a real need, the leader can easily get an agreement for the troubled person to continue.

How long will the session last? In psychotherapy it has long been accepted that an individual counseling session would last sixty minutes; later came the idea of eighty to ninety minutes as the desirable time for a group session. We have settled upon a two-hour period as the best. However, not all this time is used in group interaction, as many things hold up the process. Two hours seems to be the maximum period. As Yalom says, "After about two hours a point of diminishing return is reached."[3]

We are always tempted to personify groups, and this poetic tendency may confuse our thinking; but there are certain stages in the growth and development of a group. Like the human infant, a newly born group needs some special care so it will survive infancy, childhood, and adolescence and hopefully enter a mature adulthood. Getting to maturity will involve using the principles of group dynamics that will be the focus of discussion in our next chapter.

IDEAS FOR GROUP FACILITATORS

Negotiators in management labor disputes examined videotapes of their discussions and interpreted the gestures and movements of the participants in light of the final outcome of the encounters. They concluded that body movements were often truer indicators of some people's thoughts and ideas than were their words. This is just one of the factors that led to the development of the idea of "body language." Don't make a fetish out of it. A lot of factors may complicate the interpretation. Moreover you may be able to better understand some of your group members by applying some of the ideas from the following chart.

BODY LANGUAGE

Movement	Description	Possible Meaning
Adjusting glasses	Very slowly and deliberately takes glasses off and carefully cleans the lenses, or puts the earpiece of the frame in the mouth.	Procrastination— pausing for thought— gaining time to evaluate.
Pinching bridge of nose	Closes eyes, pinches bridge of nose.	May signal self-conflict, quandary about a matter.
Sideways glance	Often takes a sideways position, body turned away.	Associated with distrusting attitude—a gesture of rejection.

Movement	Description	Possible Meaning
Hands on hips	Standing—Both hands placed on hips. Sitting—Body leaning forward, one hand on knees.	Individual is goal-oriented—is ready and able.
Leaning back, hands supporting head	Seated, leaning back, one leg crossed in figure-four position, both hands clasped behind head.	Gesture of superiority, smugness, and authority.
Jingling money in pocket	Jingling coins in pocket.	May be much concerned with money or the lack of it.
Locked ankles	Ankles crossed tightly; hands may also be clenched.	Holding back strong feelings and emotions—apprehension—tension.
Tugging ear	Raises hand four to six inches, hand goes to earlobe, gives a subtle pull, then returns to its starting point.	An "interrupt gesture"—a signal of a wish to speak.
Steepling	Joins finger tips and forms a "church steeple."	Communicates idea of being very sure of what one is saying.
Smiles: Simple	Lips together, teeth unexposed.	Person is not participating in any outgoing activity, is similing to him or herself.
Upper	Upper incisors exposed, usually with eye-to-eye contact between individuals.	A greeting smile when friends meet—or when children greet their parents.
Broad	Both upper and lower incisors exposed and eye-to-eye contact seldom occurs.	Associated with laughing, commonly seen during play.

Movement	Description	Possible Meaning
Holding hands	Two women gently hold the other's hands in theirs and with congruous facial expressions communicate their deep sympathy.	Woman's expression of sincere feelings to another woman during a crisis.
Open hands	Palms up.	Sincerety and openness.
Crossed arms	Men—arms crossed on chest. Women—arms crossed lower on body.	Defensiveness, defiance, withdrawal.
Leg over chair	Sits with one leg up over chair arm.	Indifference or hostility to others' feelings or needs.
Leg kicking	Legs crossed with foot moving in a slight kicking motion.	Boredom.
Hand to cheek	"The thinker" position, with hand on cheek.	Involved in some sort of meditation.
Stroking chin	Hand strokes chin—man strokes beard or mustache.	In process of making decision.

≋ 10. The Dynamics of an Integrity Therapy Group

THE WORD *dynamic* is generally used in psychology to indicate change; that is, a dynamic situation is flexible rather than fixed or rigid. *Dynamic* comes from the Greek word *dunamis,* which means power or force. All too frequently this has implied an explosive force, as in the word *dynamite.* As the word is used in the phrase *group dynamics,* a more apt image is that of the force contained in a balloon full of water. I close my hand on this balloon and it squeezes through my fingers in all sorts of odd shapes, requiring careful management.

The analogy of water suggests interesting possibilities. Water can be impounded for flood control and irrigation, bringing protection from inundations and literally fulfilling Isaiah's prophecy that the desert would blossom as a rose. But it also has the potential for destruction, as was seen in the 1976 collapse of the ill-fated Teton dam, which inundated 400,000 acres of land and left nine people dead, three thousand homeless, and $1 billion of property destroyed.

Group forces have similar potential for good or ill. In the Integrity Therapy group the skillful leader seeks to direct the forces of the group for healing human hurt, in the process utilizing at least ten activities in the management of dynamics. These will be considered in turn.

THE COVENANT OF CONFIDENTIALITY

All types of counseling recognize the necessity of complete confidentiality for counseling sessions. Unless all participants understand that the session is completely private, it is unlikely that the interchange will go beyond a superficial level. For this reason some counselors are less than enthusiastic about tape recording, or even taking extensive notes, in a counseling interview.

The question of confidentiality is more complicated in group therapy, where people discuss very personal aspects of their lives before as many as ten people. Newcomers unfamiliar with Integrity Therapy are sometimes surprised at the frankness of the group discussions. The uninitiated may be fascinated with the whole procedure and may feel a burning desire to share some juicy morsel with outside friends: "The strangest thing happened in the therapy group. . . ."

Anticipating this problem, Integrity Therapy insists that group life can proceed only on the basis of absolute confidentiality. A phrase commonly used is that everybody coming into the group enters upon a *covenant of confidentiality;* that is, all the members are committed to secrecy and have an obligation to refrain from repeating anything said in a group session.

Another way of expressing this commitment is a saying frequently heard among group members, "We do not confess for somebody else." Members are at liberty to discuss their own failures and shortcomings but must leave it to others to tell their own stories. One of the subtlest ways of confessing for somebody else is to name a partner. For instance, Jill Harris says, ". . . Harry Sixtus had been a friend of ours for years, and he was always attentive and saying nice things to me. He kept after me until I became involved in an affair with him." She has effectively told the group about Harry's failure, mentioned him by name, and placed a good proportion of the blame on him. In such situations the leader will frequently say, "Never mind about giving us his name, just tell us what you did."

Members of an Integrity Therapy group are introduced on a first-name basis; their last name is not thought to be important. Thus within the group they have at least an element of anonymity. Some groups commence their sessions with a statement by the leader about the convenant of confidentiality, and during the course of the meeting the group may be periodically warned about the importance of abiding by the covenant. Anyone not keeping the covenant may be asked to leave.

THE PARTICIPATION PRINCIPLE

There is something about the term *group therapy* that excites the interest and imagination of many people, who would love the opportunity to observe a "real live therapy group." Sometimes such interest is the legitimate outcome of studies of psychology or sociology, or a genuine interest in learning how to help people, but it can also be just the activity of a psychological "peeping Tom." The intrustion of a merely curious individual puts group members at a disadvantage, giving them the impression that their psyches are open for display to any visitor's prying eyes.

No doubt many people could gain from observing a therapy group in action—Raymond J. Corsini writing on role playing refers to this as spectator therapy. The fundamental principle of Integrity Therapy, however, is expressed in the widely used statement, "no spectators, only participators." A group member who fails to participate may be asked to leave.

Participation is more than gossiping, chattering, or lecturing the other people in the group, as seen in this hypothetical case: Mary Joe Sims has joined a group and been given the warning that there are no spectators, only participators. As she listens to Jeanie Binginton relate her difficulties with her husband, Mary Joe's eyes light up. She leans forward eagerly. She can hardly wait. The moment Jeanie pauses, Mary Joe launches into a long lecture, telling Jeanie just what she should do. The leader steps in to clarify what is meant by participating and says, "Thank you, Mary Joe. I should have explained to you before that we do not start telling other people what to do until we acknowledge our own failures. We start with ourselves first before we give instruction to others."

Another way of establishing this principle is to insist any person must "earn the right" to tell another group member what to do. Members earn the right by being willing to discuss their own failures.

The participation principle has a sound theoretical basis. Integrity therapy sees at least part of peoples' difficulties as arising from separation from others. In covering up their failures, they have isolated themselves and built a barrier that must be broken down if they are to function at a meaningful level; to allow them to not participate would be doing an injustice.

THE OPENNESS POSTULATE

All types of therapy include some form of confession. Some techniques have gone to extremes in devising ingenious ways by which people can take off their masks and talk about themselves as they really are. It is anticipated in therapy that counselees will discuss matters they would probably not talk about in polite society. As William James says it, "In confession we exteriorize our rottenness."[1] In an Integrity Therapy experience participants must be willing to talk about all the areas of their lives.

The newcomer to an Integrity Therapy group is given a booklet describing the distinctive of confession in this particular form of counseling.

1. Because it is easy but self-defeating to put on a front and not acknowledge who one is, it is necessary to drop all pretenses. This is best done by confession.

2. While confession may be initially made to just one person, it should then move out in everwidening circles of personal transparency and sincerity.

3. Confession is not made indiscriminately but to significant others.

4. Complaining or blaming others for one's troubles is not confession.

5. We have no right to confess other people's shortcomings but should concentrate on our own.

6. Boasting about our virtues is not confession; confession should focus on our weaknesses rather than our strengths.

7. Confession is an indication that we are willing to come under the judgment of our fellows.[2]

Despite these guidelines, confessions may be inadequate. The easiest way of all to confess is to say, "I failed," or "I goofed," or "Of course everybody has made mistakes," or "We had an affair." Alcoholics Anonymous insists that alcoholics "admit the exact nature" of their failure. Step Four of the Twelve Steps says, "[We] made a searching and fearless moral inventory of ourselves." The Big Book of A.A. emphasizes that this inventory should be honest, thorough, and written. When some people can bring themselves to follow this step, they begin to face the realities of their own behavior. If they simply generalize, they may make no progress.

Openness is particularly important in marriage therapy. Partners in marriage are particularly vulnerable to closing off the channels of communication. They may do this by flying into a rage, arguing with a spouse, giving their partners the silent treatment, or using any of a dozen other devices to cut them off. In group interaction they have to learn how to set up channels of communication. The theory of Integrity Therapy insists that secretiveness brings on most of the difficulties in a marriage. From being open with each other in the early days of the marriage, the partners gradually become more secretive and unwilling to discuss the irritations of their life together.' Naturally enough, they are particularly reticent about their own failures. Within a group they are given an opportunity to show themselves as they really are.

Although confession sometimes seems a difficult and traumatic experience, it may be otherwise. For many people it is a relief to give up a secret that has been carried for so long. As Carl Jung says, "In keeping the matter private . . . I still continue in my state of isolation. It is only with the help of confession that I am able to throw myself into the arms of humanity, freed at last from the burden of moral exile."

THE AUDIENCE EFFECT

Some widely accepted ideas of group therapy have come directly from novels, movies, or television, which choose the most dramatic episodes of a therapy session and sometimes convey the impression that it is characteristically a highly emotional affair. People shout at each other, tear their own or others' hair, or bump heads on the floor.

All therapy groups are not the same. Undoubtedly some do function on the theory that emotion must be released. At some of these, noisy groups like the "encounters" of Daytop Lodge, participants are expected to react at the gut level. At its best or worst, according to one's perspective, the period provides an opportunity for members to pour out their hostility; the most ready defense is for other members to respond in like manner, and the final outcome appears to rest in lung power and one person's ability to outshout the other.

At Integrity Therapy groups, by contrast, voluble members or aggressive cross-examiners are reminded of the importance of listening. Listening to troubled people helps to build a good relationship with them, and allows them to break out of their isolation, to exteriorize their thoughts, and as they talk, to say something to themselves.

Communication involves listening as well as speaking. While a silent spouse may sometimes cause problems, the crux of many more matrimonial difficulties is in partners' unwillingness to listen to each other. Within their respective groups, husbands and wives will learn to listen and pay attention to what other people say; if they engage in side conversations and don't listen, they may be reproved and urged to pay more attention to the proceedings.

It has long been acknowledged that listening is a fundamental skill in individual one-to-one counseling. It is no less important in the activities of group counseling.

CREATIVE CONFRONTATION

No matter how fortuitous their experiences might have been, most people have a feeling that they missed out somewhere. It sometimes seems that the more material privileges some people have, the greater their sense of emotional deprivation. Thus nearly everybody has a ready-made excuse for poor behavior.

Psychologists haven't always helped us. Much of their investigation and theorizing looks back to the events of early life for an understanding of later development. An extreme form of this concept says, "The drama of life is but a repetition of the plot of infancy." As valuable as this type of theorizing may be for guiding child rearing and education, it may give rise to a strange fatalism. Troubled people may accept their difficulties as an inevitable and unchangeable consequence of early years, and thus be deprived of all motivation to change.

Integrity Therapy acknowledges the vital influence of the early years on personality development but hastens to point out that these influences are in the past, over and done with, and cannot be changed. They may have been unfortunate, but we cannot live under the shadow of them for the rest of our days. A common expression is, "We cannot accept good reasons for bad behavior."

One common rationalization is to make vices out of virtues. Mrs. Skeen is talking about herself and trying to understand where she has failed. She has a large family and nurses deep resentments toward her husband. With a martyred look on her face and a tear in her voice she says, "I guess my problem is that I am just too sweet. I let them walk all over me as if I were a door mat."

She looks sadly around the group waiting for their sympathy and commendation.

But Charlotte Ford won't let her get away with it. "That's not a failing; it's a virtue. I wish I had the capacity for long-suffering. Tell us about your weaknesses."

People who rationalize by blaming others for their difficulties also become targets for the rest of the group. Jim Jones tells how badly his wife Mary keeps house, neglects him, and squanders his money. He soon discovers he is wasting his time. The group says, "We don't have Mary here so we cannot do anything to her. Never mind about what she did. Where did you fail?"

Any type of counseling that emphasizes responsibility necessarily engages in some form of confrontation. In Gestalt therapy, for example, when members of the group say, "I can't," the therapist asks them to change "I can't" to "I won't." The idea is give the subject the sense of being in charge of the situation; saying "I won't" means one is a responsible person who is in the driver's seat and really has control of the situation.

In *Basic Types of Pastoral Counseling,* Howard J. Clinebell, Jr. places Integrity Therapy under the general heading of confrontational counseling. The classification may be misleading if the reader gets the image of a group bearing down on one of the members in a relentless cross-examination. Such is seldom the case. Integrity Therapy groups are generally willing to let people talk, to listen to them, and to offer support. Nevertheless, there are some moments when they confront members with aspects of their experience where individual responsibility must be faced.

THE IDENTIFICATION PROCESS

In the course of these sessions of group interaction, members are exposed to accounts of other people's struggles with life. Listening to others recounting the story of the difficulties they faced, the bad moves they made, the outcomes of self-defeating actions, listeners frequently come to see their own dilemmas in a clearer light.

John tells the story of his drinking problem. He realizes it is ruining his marriage. His wife and family can only take so much. He relates his feeling of disgust when he looks back on one of his drinking episodes. Then he goes ahead and does it again. Jim, seated on the other side of the room, listens to the story, then says, "That's exactly what I do." This experience helps to remove John's awful feeling of isolation. There is someone else who is passing through a similar experience and understands his particular difficulties. It may be that John has found a better way of approaching the problem.

The suspicion of professionals that characterizes many self-help movements may stem from their insistence that like speak to like. In Alcoholics Anonymous the alcoholic helps a drinking friend; in Seven Steppers an exconvict works with the prisoner; in Recovery the mental hospital patient provides assistance for the newly released patient; in Daytop Lodge the exaddict helps addicts. In such groups there is a strong sense of camaraderie, which supports the perplexed seeker for help. As members of Integrity Therapy say, "We are all strugglers together in the sea of life."

Some people are overwhelmed by a sense of self-pity. When they are isolated from other people, they build their problems up in their minds to ridiculous proportions. When they come to a group and hear people talk, they suddenly discover someone worse off than themselves. Sometimes they say, "Before I came here I thought I had problems, but after hearing these other people I realize my difficulties are really ever so small. I didn't realize how well-off I was."

Among the groups there are generally a few people exhibiting severe problems. Newcomers may be threatened by the talk of a group member who is hallucinating or delusional. However, such an experience may be valuable if it shocks them into reasoning that they had better watch out or they will get into a similar state. It may provide a motivation for working harder on their own difficulties.

In one highly dramatic form of psychotherapy called *psychodrama*, participants act out their problem with other people. In an effective Integrity Therapy group the same effect is gained in another way. It is as if participants were watching their own behavior being acted out on stage by some other person. As onlookers they are able to assess this behavior in someone else, and so are able to make a more objective evaluation of their own behavior.

THE DIALOGICAL RESPONSE

Members of a group react to each other—it isn't very long before they are talking back and forth. Although an Integrity Therapy group is under the direction of a leader, wise leaders do not interfere when they see the group engaged in dialogue. When leaders are most effective, it sometimes seems as if their presence is almost unnecessary.

Harriet is anxious. She went to work in an office and gradually advanced until she became secretary to the boss. He was very nice to her—he took her to lunch, brought little gifts back from his trips, gave her extra time off. One night they went to a company banquet and on the way home they stopped off at his lake house, where they became sexually involved.

Harriet looks at her husband Charles, who has not been successful in any of his business ventures. He is unromantic and stodgy compared with her free-spending boss. She concludes that Charles will never make it in the stiff competition of the business world. If they want some of the nicer things in life, she must face the prospect of working in the office for the rest of her days.

Harriet grows increasingly anxious. While taking dictation one day, she bursts into tears, and this leads to a showdown with her boss. He talks very gently and tells her how important she is to him; however, there are many facts that must be faced. He is married, with three children, and at this advanced stage of his marriage he sees no possibility of a divorce. So he makes an offer to Harriet. If she wants to leave her husband, he will rent an apartment for her and give her a substantial advance in salary. Harriet is tempted to accept this offer.

In her anxiety, and not knowing which way to turn, she has come to the counseling center, where she is given an opportunity to join a group. She tells her story to the women in her group. No sooner is she finished talking than Susan, another group member, tells of her experience in a similar situation. Her boss did even better than Harriet's: he offered to marry her. She divorced her rather stodgy husband and married the flamboyant boss. Now there is all sorts of trouble with him. As her boss he was charming; as her husband he is unbearable. She suspects he might be repeating his previous behavior with his present secretary. She simply doesn't trust him.

Susan and Harriet discuss the pros and cons of the situation. The dialogue that follows gives Harriet food for thought as she comes to see two sides of the question.

In this experience of dialogue the members often counsel one another. Looking at the problem from a perspective similar to that of the troubled person, they are able to offer helpful counsel from their personal experience. This is one of the secrets of self-help groups.

RAISING ALTERNATIVES

One of the most important functions of any group activity is helping individuals grasp the reality of their situations. Anxiety frequently makes people think they face an impasse from which there is no escape; capitulation is inevitable. But frequently there is some aspect that has not been considered, and the group helps make it possible to sort out the issues and clarify the alternatives.

Charlene is telling the other people in the group about her situation. Her husband has some good points, but he is so domineering that she just can't stand him. Because she bought a piece of furniture without consulting him, he blew his top and a terrible scene ensued. He fussed for hours, and for a while she feared he might do her bodily harm. For her this is the last straw. She is going to divorce him. There is no other way.

Linda, the group leader who has had wide experience, says, "Let's explore some of the possibilities and try to see what will be the probable outcome of your plan of action." Turning to the group she says, "What does everyone else think?"

Martha, glad to have her husband home again after difficulties in the past, suggests "You can stay with him and learn to put up with his annoying ways."

Jean, the veteran of three divorces, quietly comments, "You can divorce him and go free; but what will happen to your children? How will they get along without a father?"

Johnnie Lou speaks up, "How will you live? What sort of work can you do?"

Other members chime in to tell of their or others' experiences in these situations.

People in the group with such varied backgrounds offer a remarkable number of alternatives and possibilities. While the group will not make decisions for people, it helps them see the real issues that must be considered before an adequate conclusion can be reached.

THE RICOCHET EFFECT

The "ricochet effect" is seen in groups where the leader is aware of a group member who needs to face a situation but is unwilling to participate. The leader involves other members of the group with somewhat similar situations in an analysis of their problems. As the interaction continues, the nonparticipating member may be compelled to face his or her own situation.

Tom Hawkins has a sales position that periodically requires him to work long hours into the evening, giving him a ready-made excuse for absences from home. He and his wife were married very young, and now he is moving in a more sophisticated crowd. He feels his wife has not kept up with him, and he pays less attention to her. She and their little boy are left by themselves for increasingly long periods of time.

When the showdown finally comes and his wife demands an explanation for his absences, Tom announces he wants a divorce. He says there is no other woman, but in fact he has become interested in a divorcée. To his wife his whole argument is that he is just tired of the responsibilities of married life and wants his freedom.

In the intake interview Tom reveals he was a psychology major in college and has done graduate work in counseling. He has decided that he will beat the interviewer at the game. He politely says the only reason he has come is that his wife has said she will not even consider giving him a divorce until he has consulted a counselor.

During this cagey interview Tom half-heartedly admits that he has not been a good husband. He feels he was married too young. It isn't really necessary for him to stay out as late as he does at night, but he just doesn't want to go home. He enjoys more sophisticated company.

When invited to join a group, he says he is not interested. Pressed a little, he puts his attitude in the best light by saying that if he came to the group, it would only build up his wife's vain hopes of rehabilitating the marriage, which would not be fair. In the last moments of the interview he decides he will give it a try, but Tom is obviously a poor prospect for a group whose primary emphasis is openness and acceptance of responsibility.

During the week before the group meeting, Tom announces to his wife that he has no intention of really attending the meeting. The tearful wife, on the telephone for forty-five minutes with her group leader, pours out her fears and apprehensions. She is counseled to take it easy and realize this is part of a "war of nerves."

Tom comes to the group meeting, but his every posture and gesture fairly shout apathy and disinterest. In the "hopes and fears" session he says he came under duress and intended to outsmart the other group members.

The leader wisely leaves Tom on one side and makes no attempt to draw him into the discussion. He does everything to convey the impression that Tom is just a spectator and, as soon as possible, leads Charlie to talk. A handsome man in his early thirties, Charles had left home some six weeks before. From an earlier conversation the counselor knows he is sick of his lonely life and also feels a little guilty about ducking the responsibility for his children.

Nearby sits Gene, also separated from his wife. He too is not happy about it all. Although he had walked out on her, he was now having second thoughts. He was just about to decide to go back home and try it again.

As the leader guides the discussion, he leads the two men to talk about the loneliness of life away from home. They laugh as they make cracks about the sorry food they now live on and contrast it with the home-cooked meals they used to enjoy. The leader quizzes them about their responsibility to their children and their wives. "How do you feel about children who didn't ask to be born but were brought into the world by your volition? How do you think it feels for a boy growing up without the love and attention of a father? Is love just being attracted to a pretty face or a sexy figure? Don't we have some obligation to keep a marriage vow?"

Not one word is spoken to Tom during the two-hour session. The leader apparently ignores him, but in reality he is using the ricochet effect, bouncing ideas off Charlie and Gene, who are thus innocently counseling Tom.

CLARIFYING VALUES

It is sometimes said that some types of therapy lower the client's values by pointing out that guilt is unnecessary. Integrity Therapy, on the other hand, is said to stress raising the individual's guilt level; in fact, it is a technique for increasing guilt. However, this is not an accurate evaluation of the emphasis. It would be more accurate to say that Integrity Therapy aims to help individuals discover and clarify their own values.

After hearing individuals talk about their ideas of right and wrong, good and bad, we sometimes feel we understand their values. However, we may not have an inkling what their values really are, because many values are held unconsciously. It may take some form of group interaction, a period of introspection, or a crisis to bring awareness of one's true values.

Values can be divided into two categories: conceived values and practiced values. Practiced values are the behavior patterns generally observed, but conceived values may be the most important. No matter how people live, they still have an idea of the way life *should* be lived. They may see their own behavior as a concession to the imperfect world in which they live.

On a muggy July night in 1977, lightning delivered a quadruple blow to the Con Edison's electricity system, and by 9:40 P.M. nine million New Yorkers were plunged into darkness as a result of what a Con Edison spokesman described as an "act of God." In the twenty-five hours that followed, it was not the acts of God but human acts that became the focal point, as under the anonymity of darkness looters pillaged some two thousand places of business. The estimate of property loss ran up to $1 million.

Under the cover of darkness values took a beating. One teenage girl struggling along with a load of stolen clothes and radios met some boys who offered to help her carry her load. As soon as they gained possession they deserted her and made off with the loot. The girl complained to her friends, "That's not right. They shouldn't have done that." In other words, it was all right for her to steal the goods but entirely wrong for someone else to steal from her.

In an Integrity Therapy group, troubled people are compelled to take a long and penetrating look at their values. The group members challenge them and insist they justify their position.

Deborah is on the defensive. She has acknowledged that her husband works hard and makes a good living. He provides her with a housekeeping allowance, and by cutting corners and economizing she is able to save $50 a month, which she sends to a favorite nephew who is having financial difficulties. Her husband thinks her nephew is a wastrel and refuses to help him. Naturally Deborah doesn't want her husband to know about the monthly remittances.

One of the group speaks up to ask if this is not a deceptive way of doing things. In a spirited defense Deborah maintains that if she manages carefully and is able to save $50 from her housekeeping money, it is hers to do with as she wishes. She is adamant; nothing can change her mind.

The weeks pass. Although the group is wary about Deborah's sensitive reaction, finances are frequently discussed. Week by week the group bats the subject back and forth, and along with it they discuss the problems deception brings in marriage.

Finally there comes an evening when, in the course of the discussion, Deborah is asked directly about her housekeeping budget. She grins. "Would you believe I've changed my mind about the money being mine?"

The group smiles as she tells of the change of attitude that led her to tell her husband what she had been doing. After a long talk about it all, her husband convinced her it wasn't good strategy to send the money. She is now putting the $50 aside each month for their annual vacation.

Within the group Deborah had been led to reconsider her behavior. In this experience she learned to recognize her true values. It is not that the group moralizes. Sermons have no place. Rather, the constant demand is that participants clarify their own values and decide how they should behave in consideration of their true values.

THE ACTIVITY EXPECTATION

Different types of therapy emphasize different aspects of personality. Some therapies focus on the intellectual area of human experience—as rational creatures, people need to see the illogic of their behavior. Therapy consists in helping them make an intellectual evaluation of what they have done. When they have insight and come to understand the why of their behavior, they are ready to move on to new and better levels of living.

Other types of therapy—and these are in the majority—stress the emotional side of life. Traumatic experiences have thrown up emotional blockages, which have immobilized the intellectual processes and left the sufferer in a sorry state. These theories emphasize the expression of emotion, and therapy becomes a means of catharsis to release the pent-up emotional forces and let the individual act in a sensible way.

In contrast to both types of techniques, Integrity Therapy stresses action. This emphasis stems partly from the realization that it is virtually impossible to change emotions. About the only way to bring about an alteration in feelings is to utilize some type of chemical agent, but the use of drugs is not the province of the psychotherapist. In one of the favorite expressions of Integrity Therapy, "It is much easier to act yourself into a new way of feeling than to feel yourself into a new way of acting."

The challenge is not, "How do you feel?" but rather "What did you do?" The most frequently asked question is, "How have you been behaving yourself?" Group members learn early to look for bad moves they have made. In explaining their situation they say, "I got into trouble because I made the wrong moves."

The way out of these difficulties is action. There is no sympathy with people who feel depressed and imagine they are physically weak and that the best way of handling their depression is to lie around. The insistence is that they get up and get moving and become involved in a plan of action.

Not activity for activity's sake. Alcoholics Anonymous has called for a return to the idea of restitution in the steps that say they "made a list of all persons we had harmed and became willing to make amends to them," and "made direct amends to such people whenever possible, except when to do so would injure them or others." Integrity Therapy Groups give assignments to their members in some way equal to their perceived area of failure. The rationale behind such assignments is that people pay for their guilt with their symptoms and bring misery upon themselves and others, and so they must learn new ways of behaving so that guilt will be paid for in a constructive manner.

Working on the premise that conscience is the internalized voice of society, the Integrity Therapy group becomes the representative of that wider society. Consequently, the group can lay responsibility upon the individual to undertake some type of repayment, or putting back into life.

Assignments take various forms. In husband-wife relationships the wife might be told to clean her refrigerator, take time to fix her hair, or undertake some task to help another person. The husband might be given the assignment of expressing his love to his wife, spending specified periods of time with his children, or undertaking some neglected work around the house. Individuals may also be given an opportunity to decide on their own assignments.

The stress on activity is so strong that Integrity Therapy is sometimes called an action therapy. Action brings with it a sense being able to *do something* in the dilemma that seems to have overwhelmed the subject.

FOSTERING COMMITMENT

Any type of communal or group activity calls for some type of commitment. In one fine study of communes, *Community and Commitment* (Cambridge: Harvard University Press, 1972), Rosabeth Moss Kahter describes the mechanisms used in successful communes to build a sense of commitment to the enterprise. A similar commitment is build within an individual who, after living an irresponsible life, comes to join an Integrity Therapy group.

O. Hobart Mowrer is fond of saying that Integrity groups are both the quickest and the slowest way of handling a crisis in life. They are the quickest because becoming open, accepting responsibility, undertaking restitution, and getting involved in a group sometimes provide a nearly miraculous release. But these groups are also the slowest because the experience within the group that brings so much relief at its best entails a commitment to a whole new way of life.

Mowrer's attitude is characteristic of self-help groups, but it has caused some difficulties with certain self-helpers. Synanon, which has been so effective in working with drug addicts, indicates that once people become members of their organization, there is a possibility they may never leave again. They will continue to function within the organization, finding fulfillment in what they are doing. This may even involve a permanent residence within the organization. Synanon explains that it is not an institution but a way of life; consequently there is no reason for anyone to leave what has become a fulfilling existence.

Alcoholics Anonymous does not require people to live in a residence, but may call for a commitment to the enterprise that keeps the alcoholic very busy. Some critics charge that alcoholics replace addiction to alcohol with addiction to meetings, as A.A. members find themselves committed to a constant round of group meetings. They are also committed to help other people—the common saying is, "You cannot keep your experience unless you give it away."

Sometimes newcomers to an Integrity Therapy group will ask, "How long will it take me to get through this?" in much the same manner that a prospective student asks about the duration of a course. Behind this inquiry is the hope that they will be told, "You may need to come for a month or two months." But those involved in any type of group therapy discover that it is a long process. Some group therapies tell people it will be at least a year and a half before they can expect to leave the group. New members of Integrity Therapy groups are asked to commit themselves for a least six weeks, but this period of time is specified so that they will not feel discouraged. But if the interviewer were really honest, the answer might be, "You may never leave the groups again."

After six weeks in an Integrity Therapy group, members will sometimes announce, "Well, I've finished my six weeks. I guess that's all I need." To such a statement the response is, "What about all these other people who need help? Aren't you going to do something about them?" Then the proposition is put to them that they might become helpers and learn to work as assistants in groups. Altruism has been found to be one of the curative factors in a group—through helping others, members discover new strength for themselves.

This new responsibility may be an important part of the total program of therapy from many points of view. One unanticipated outcome of participation in a group has been the discovery of hitherto unrealized leadership skills. Many people who come originally as counselees have become group leaders and then gone on to become outstanding leaders in community endeavors. Some have been so successful that they have become professional leaders of social service agencies.

A recent biography of President Lyndon Baines Johnson highlighted the president's need for company. He had push button phones everywhere; at his Texas ranch he had thirteen speakers strategically placed so he could be heard in every part of the property. He was never away from radio or television. His office had a three-screen television console, so that he could watch all three network news sessions simultaneously, as well as the tickers of the major news wire services. Johnson said, "These tickers were like friends tapping at my door for attention. They made me feel I was in the center of things. I could stand beside these tickers for hours on end and never get lonely."[3]

One does not have to be the president of the United States nor be able to afford electronic gadgetry to escape isolation and loneliness. There are few experiences that can bring the satisfaction that comes from leading a group and sensing the dynamics that bring to a troubled spirit the message, "You need never be lonely again."

Epilogue

WHO'S AFRAID of the self-help groups? Many people. Professionals have been particularly defensive, perhaps from the threat they see in the techniques of self-helpers. As Nathan Hurvitz, himself a professional, has said:

> It is important to recognize that Peer Self-Help Psychotherapy Groups achieve their goals without application of specific behavior modification techniques, without an existential search for identity, without the exploration of human potential, without awareness training to actualize one's potential, without the analysis of the transference neurosis, without psychodrama, without clearing engrams, without creative fighting, without mind expanding drugs, without sensory awakening, without marathons, without feeling each other up, without taking off their clothes, and without sexual intercourse between therapists and clients.[1]

Church leaders have been just as inhospitable, despite the fact that the principles of the self-helpers bear a close resemblance to those enunciated in the New Testament and practiced by the early church. Honesty, openness, and involvement would seem to be the most obvious qualities to be developed within church life, yet all too frequently a church leader will respond, "You couldn't possibly have that in church, the news would spread around the community." The fear of gossip may be part of what the church is suffering from. But churches ought to be places where we can be ourselves and acknowledge our failures and shortcomings.

The community at large is often afraid of the self-helpers, apparently because sexual indiscretions might be mentioned. This is quite ironic in a society that has spent so much of its time exploiting human sexuality through X-rated movies, pornographic literature, and so on.

Fortunately some people are not afraid of the self-help groups:

Alcoholics who were at the end of their tether find a whole new way of life in a caring community. Drug addicts who went to the clinics and hospitals and came away with a shot of methadone find deliverance in groups of exaddicts.

Criminals who were full of resentment about the iniquities of the legal system they saw as loaded against them learn in a group of exconvicts new ways of coming to terms with society and living a free and meaningful life.

The depressed and frustrated who spent long years of darkness and despair in a drug-clouded world find new pathways to an optimistic outlook on life.

The husband and wife who spent their days in a running battle, futilely blaming each other, through sessions with their peers learn new and meaningful ways of relating to each other and to the other members of their family.

It is true that self-helpers are not always the best company—they may not be well rounded, and their thoughts run on a single track—but we desperately need them in our society. No need to fear the self-helpers. Let us welcome them, study them, understand them, and, above everything else, emulate them.

Notes

INTRODUCTION

1. J. H. Powell, *Bring Out Your Dead* (New York: Time, Inc., 1965), p. xiv.
2. O. Hobart Mowrer, Anthony J. Vattano, et al., *Integrity Groups: The Loss and Recovery of Community* (Urbana, Ill.: Integrity Groups, 1975), p. 140.
3. Mowrer and Vattano, pp. 140
4. Mowrer and Vattano, p. 265.
5. Mowrer and Vattano, p. 266.
6. Mowrer and Vattano, pp. 254–263
7. Cited in Mowrer and Vattano, pp. 260–261.
8. Fort Worth *Star Telegram,* June 15, 1976.

CHAPTER 1

1. Nehemiah Curnock, ed., *The Journal of the Rev. John Wesley, A. M.,* (London: Epworth Press, 1909), 3:38–39 (hereafter referred to as *Journal*).
2. Rev. L. Tyerman, *The Life and Times of the Rev. John Wesley, A.M.,* I (London: Hodder and Stoughton, 1870), p. 121.
3. *Journal,* 1:458.
4. *Journal,* 2:50.
5. John Telford, ed., *The Letters of Rev. John Wesley, A.M.,* (London: Epworth Press, 1931), vol. II, p. 10.

CHAPTER 2

1. *The Works of John Wesley, A.M.,* 3rd ed. (London: Wesleyan Methodist Book Room), 8:302 (hereafter referred to as *Works*).
2. *Works,* 13:255.
3. *Works,* 8:250.
4. *Works,* 13:250.
5. *Works,* 1:416.
6. *Works,* 8:255.
7. *Works,* 8:301. ("Leadership" discussed in a number of places in *Works*.)
8. Peter Donald MacKenzie, *The Methodist Class Meeting: A Historical Study* (Saint Andrews: Thesis for Master of Theology, Saint Andrews University, 1969), p. 47.

9. MacKenzie, p. 31.
10. *Works,* 8:260.
11. *Works,* 8:307.
12. John Telford, ed., *The Letters of the Rev. John Wesley, A.M.* (London: The Edworth Press, 1960), 7:47.

CHAPTER 3

1. Tom Driberg, *The Mystery of Moral Re-Armament* (New York: Alfred A. Knopf, 1965), p. 20.
2. Walter Houston Clark, *The Oxford Group, Its History and Significance* (New York: Bookman Associates, 1951), p. 168.
3. Clark, p. 28.
4. Clark, p. 64–65.
5. Peter Howard, "The Result is a Miracle." In O. Hobart Mowrer, ed., *Morality and Mental Health* (Chicago: Rand McNally, 1967), p. 626.
6. Clark, p. 68.
7. Clark, p. 70.
8. Alcoholics Anonymous, *Twelve Steps and Twelve Traditions* (New York: Alcoholics World Services, Inc., 1955), pp. 59–60.
9. Alcoholics Anonymous, p. 60.
10. *Meet Neurotics Anonymous* (Washington, D.C.: Neurotics Anonymous International Liaison, Inc., 1966).

CHAPTER 4

1. Helen Keller, *The Story of My Life* (New York: Doubleday, Doran and Company, Inc., 1963), p. 23.
2. Keller, p. 24.
3. Calvin S. Hall and Gardiner Lindzey, *Theories of Personality* (New York: John Wiley and Son, 1957), p. 134.
4. Nathan W. Ackerman, "Family Therapy." In Silvano Arieti, ed., *American Handbook of Psychiatry* (New York: Basic Books, 1966), vol. III, p. 203.
5. Irvin D. Yalom, *The Theory and Practice of Group Psychotherapy* (New York: Basic Books, 1970), p. 201.
6. John W. Drakeford, *Farewell to the Lonely Crowd* (Waco: Word Books, 1969), pp. 78–79.
7. Yalom, p. 202.
8. Yalom, pp. 70–71.
9. Harry F. Harlow and Margaret Kuenne Harlow, "Social Deprivation in Monkeys," *Scientific American Readings in Psychology* (San Francisco: W. H. Freeman, 1969), vol II, p. 499.

CHAPTER 5

1. C. J. Jung, *Modern Man in Search of a Soul* (New York: Harcourt Brace and Company, 1933), p. 35.
2. James Barke, ed., *Poems and Songs of Robert Burns* (London: Collins, 1955), p. 138.

2. Charles Nordhoff, *The Communistic Societies of the United States* (New York: Dover Publications Inc., 1966), p. 291.
4. Murray Levine and Barbara Benedict Bunker, *Mutual Criticism* (Syracuse: Syracuse University Press, 1975), p. 29–34.
5. Nordhoff, p. 293.
6. George Weinberg, *The Action Approach* (New York: World Publishing Company, 1969), p. 219.
7. Levine and Bunker, p. 94.

CHAPTER 6

1. Nathan Hurvitz, "The Characteristics of Peer Self-Help Psychotherapy Groups and Their Implications for the Theory and Practice of Psychotherapy." Mowrer & Vattano, p. 153.
2. Drakeford, *Farewell to the Lonely Crowd* (Waco, Texas: Word Books, 1969), p. 238.
3. Lewis Yablonsky, *Synanon: The Tunnel Back* (Baltimore: Penguin Books, 1967), p. 175.
4. Mowrer and Vattano, p. 237.
5. Yablonsky, pp. 258–259.
6. Ester S. Manz, *How to Take Off Pounds Sensibly* (Milwaukee: TOPS Club, Inc., 1965), pp. 16–17.
7. Bill D. Schul, "Seven Steps to Freedom," *These Times*, October, 1966.
8. Mowrer and Vattano, p. 238.
9. William James, *The Varieties of Religious Experience* (New York: Longmans, Green and Co., 1929), p. 463.
10. Yablonsky, p. 185.
11. Yablonsky, p. 94.
12. Yablonsky, p. 259.

CHAPTER 7

1. Drakeford, *Farewell to the Lonely Crowd*, p. 74.
2. Drakeford, *The Little Red Book* (privately printed, Fort Worth, Texas).
3. Albert Bandura, *Principles of Behavior Modification* (New York: Holt Rinehart and Winston, Inc., 1969), p. 144.
4. Yalom, p. 94.
5. O. Hobart Mowrer, *Abnormal Reactions or Actions?* (Dubuque, Iowa: Wm. C. Brown, 1966), p. 24.
6. *The Discoverer*, vol. 4, no. 2 (publication of I. T. Now defunct).

CHAPTER 9

1. Mowrer and Vattano, p. 66.
2. Mowrer and Vattano, pp. 63–65.
3. Yalom, p. 210.

CHAPTER 10

1. William James, p. 462.
2. Drakeford, *Little Red Book.*
3. *Book Digest* (October 1976): 38.

EPILOGUE

1. Mowrer and Vattano, p. 151.

Index